THE
COURAGE
TO LOVE

THE COURAGE TO LOVE

REKINDLING THE MAGIC OF RELATIONSHIPS

MALCOLM STERN &
SUJATA BRISTOW

PIATKUS

© 1996 Malcolm Stern and Sujata Bristow

Published in 1996 by
Judy Piatkus (Publishers) Limited
5 Windmill Street
London W1P 1HF

The moral right of the authors has been asserted

A catalogue record for this book is available from the British Library

ISBN 0–7499–1646–X

Edited by Kelly Davis
Designed by Sue Ryall

Typeset by Phoenix Photosetting, Lordswood, Chatham, Kent
Printed and bound in Great Britain by
Biddles Ltd, Guildford & King's Lynn

Contents

Acknowledgments

We would both like to acknowledge the support and encouragement of Judy Piatkus, Gill Cormode and especially our editor, Kate Callaghan, whose enthusiasm has kept us on course through the difficult times. We would also like to thank the many people around whose stories the book has been woven.

I, Malcolm, want to honour and appreciate my wife, Amanda, whose wisdom is helping me find the courage to love. Our children, Michael and Alexandra, and my daughter Melissa have been ongoing teachers of spontaneity, joy and beauty.

Thanks also to my parents, Helen and Moe, who have always loved me unconditionally, and to the many friends and teachers who have shone their light on my path. I am eternally grateful to the thousands of people who have worked with me in therapy over the years, and shared the depths of their feelings. Out of these meetings, the concept of this book was born.

Sujata has been a constant and inspiring friend and co-creator. Her writing is poetic and deep, and has enabled me to share my work. I would not have been able to do so without her.

I, Sujata, would like to acknowledge the support and love of my husband, Robert. Out of the joys and the challenges of our marriage, this work has grown. Our children, Rosie and Tom, have been a continuing source of wisdom and inspiration.

I would also like to pay tribute here to the many friends who have kept me company throughout the creation of this book. And to Malcolm, my fellow traveller and dear friend, my gratitude and love.

Introduction

We all know what it is like to fall in love. Even if it has never actually happened to you, you've read the books, seen the films, heard the music. It is seen in the West as the best thing that can happen between two people. But we all know, if we have been there, that that is not the end of the story.

When we are in love, we can feel more real and alive than ever before, but we cannot stay there. Sooner or later the enchantment wears off, and our critical faculties return. We wake up to the fact that we do not really know this other person with whom we have fallen into partnership. Nor do we know who we ourselves are, any better than we did before.

MAKING A NEW MAP

It is the beginning of a long journey. We have no choice about whether or not to set out on the road, for we are all linked with other people in one way or another, and if you engage with others you will run into difficulties. We do have a choice, however, about how far and how fast we wish to travel. Our parents and grandparents gave us maps and guidelines, though they were incomplete and often contradictory; but the signposts have been moved and the landscape itself has changed. We are asking new questions of relationship these days: wanting less compromise, more intimacy, more truth; partnership in which neither takes power, and neither gives it away. For this new country, we have to make new maps for ourselves.

This book is an attempt to make such a map. It has grown out of experience rather than wishful thinking; we have tried to start, not with how we think we should be, but how we actually are. The experience we have drawn upon is our own, and that of the thousands of people who have passed through Malcolm's workshops, or been in therapy with him, since the late 1970s. His is the primary inspiration and the wealth of experience in the field of psychotherapy. From here onward, 'I' refers to Malcolm. However, this is a joint creation, and it speaks for us both. Most of the writing is Sujata's, the stories are Malcolm's, and the book has been created from a shared vision.

Our orientation is heterosexual, and this is reflected in the way we write. However, we are dealing here with issues that are common to all human relationships. Having acknowledged some of our limitations, we hope that, at least some of the time, we will be able to move beyond them.

We have called this book 'The Courage to Love', because we believe that there is a key here to much of the pain we experience in relationship. It does take courage to love, and to go on loving; to be prepared to let down our barriers and be truly vulnerable with one another. The original meaning of courage is far more than just bravery, for it comes from the medieval French, *rage du coeur*, 'the fury or passion of the heart'. This is the passion that burns through fear, that transcends our self-imposed limits and seizes life with both hands. It is this quality that we need to call upon, and to cultivate, if we are to succeed in our quest.

People come into therapy bringing their pain, their rage, their grief, their guilt, and they ask the same questions again and again. Where did it go wrong? Why don't my relationships last? How can I learn to relate better? What happened to the love that was between us? There are no prescriptions in this book, for each of us in the end has to find his or her own way, but there are guidelines and signposts, and some well-trodden paths. Besides our own experience, we have drawn upon the wisdom of people living in other times and other cultures, for one thing is certain: we need new role models for relationship in these changing times, and we must find them for ourselves.

WHY BOTHER WITH RELATIONSHIPS?

The journey of relationship is a long and perilous one, fraught with disappointments, dead ends, frustration and pain. So why should we put ourselves through all this suffering? Why not choose, as more and more people do these days, to live alone, without close ties to anyone? Or why not do as many of our parents did – and as most of us still do to some extent – and compromise, treading softly around each other, trading passion for security?

There are many answers to this question. The obvious one is that it hurts to be alone. We all have needs – for companionship, for support, for intimacy, to share experiences. In order to be alone, we must deny those needs. And when we are in relationship, we find that it also hurts to compromise. Deep in all of us there is a yearning to meet and be met, to let down the barriers, to find union. It is fear, in one or other of its guises, that holds us back.

So, just as pain drives us to withdraw, to put up barriers, it also drives us to keep trying. Here is the key to the second layer. Why bother with relationship? It is because, as living beings, we have an inbuilt urge to grow, to realise ourselves more fully. This is with us from birth until death, and resisting it causes us pain. Relating to others, especially on an intimate level, stimulates the process of growth like nothing else. This is how we are challenged, made to confront our own bad habits and expand our horizons. Relationships provide us with a vital key to self-transformation, precisely because they give us so much trouble. Through our mistakes and disasters, we are forced to grow.

When we have agreed with those close to us that relationship can work in this way, then it becomes an enormously potent tool for transformation. This is because within an intimate relationship we can create a safe environment to explore all those parts of ourselves that have been stunted, stifled and buried since childhood. And we can go beyond that, opening up the immense potential within us. If we are willing to undertake the whole journey with another, the potential for alchemy is there: the transmutation of lead into gold – of the coarse, unrealised human being into the noble one.

Here is the key to yet another layer of potential in relationship; one that we get a glimpse of when we fall in love, and perhaps at a few other exceptional moments in our lives. When we enter into partnership with another who is willing to embrace the same perspective, who has the same commitment to finding a way through the tangle of fears and neuroses that prevent us from touching each other, then we can create magic together. We can vow to keep each other awake.

In becoming awake, we realise that our lives have been lived on autopilot; so much afraid of living that we have never truly sensed the divine being within. This divine being is not a God belonging to any particular religion or sect; it is our guide and loving teacher, and the source of our yearning.

Within the magic of relationship, we can truly embrace Christ's saying that 'When two or more are gathered together in my name, there am I in the midst of them'; or the Hindu concept of *satsang*, that urges us to seek the company of like-minded people; or the words of the Buddha who, when asked what part friendship could play in the spiritual life, replied, 'Wholesome friendship is the whole of the spiritual life.' What a wonderful adventure to embark upon – perhaps the greatest adventure, in fact, that life has to offer.

How Can We Find Such Relationships?

In this book we will take a look at some of the basic skills we need to equip us for this adventure. They are not particularly complicated, nor in any way esoteric. They involve willingness to change, commitment to stay with the process of change as it unfolds, and the resolution to keep practising. We will share with you some of the tools that are working for us in our lives, and starting to make sense of this crazy existence; starting to build the structure within which the joys of heaven may be experienced on earth.

Throughout the book, we have used stories to illustrate the points being made, and to show how the people described have made changes in their lives. They are all true; only names and some other details have been changed to preserve confidentiality. Their stories provide a window into the lives and experience of other people at a level that we would ordinarily never see, except perhaps at rare moments with our closest friends.

You will find your own life mirrored here. As Jacob Moreno, the founder of Psychodrama*, said, 'We are all more alike than we are different'. If you are moved by any of these stories, if they put you in touch with your own emotions or present you with new insights, they will have served their purpose. Take what speaks to you, and use it as you will.

---

* psychodrama is a therapeutic technique which uses dramatic acting or re-enactment of difficult issues as a means to facilitate understanding, self-expression and resolution.

1

Falling in Love: Con-Trick or Divine Gift?

'It does not much signify whom one marries as one is sure to find next morning that it is someone else.'

SAMUEL ROGERS

IN THE BEGINNING

Relationship begins with falling in love. This, at least, is the expectation that we grow up with. You'll explore a little, go out with a few girls or boys, and sooner or later the magic will happen. That's how you'll know that this is the one for you, the one with whom everything is possible. Through the mists of 'happily ever after' can be glimpsed the beautiful wedding, the shared home, the children. Sexual union, the end of loneliness. Caring for each other, growing old together, knowing your place in the world because you have this one, intimate, no-holds-barred relationship where you love, and are loved, without reservation.

How many people do you know who actually do live happily ever after? When we look at our own relationships and those around us, which are the ones that survive the difficult times, and which come to grief? The plain truth is that the way the relationship begins, whether in high passion or careful calculation of its potential, or somewhere in between the two, has very little to do with its survival in the long term. What we do know for certain is

1

that the state of being 'in love' does not last. Sooner or later, the passion begins to subside, the magic wears off. What happens next? And if romantic love is not really about making relationships, then what is it about?

This chapter explores what its meaning may be, and what we can learn from romantic love, both about ourselves and about those we choose as partners. It starts by focussing on what being in love is actually like, and considering the place it may have in our emotional and spiritual lives. The journey begins with our own experience; only after looking closely at this can we move on to consider the Other, the object of our love. How do we choose a partner, and what does our choice have to show us? And finally, through becoming more aware and awake, how can we enjoy being in love to the full, whether we take it onward into relationship or not?

BEING IN LOVE: MICHAEL AND LUCY

A few years ago, I arranged a meeting between two friends of mine, Michael and Lucy, which led to their falling in love. Both were in search of partners, and I had a strong feeling that there would be a spark between them. They were well matched in many ways; both had learned from previous relationships, and were committed to their own growth. Their first contact was by phone, as they lived at opposite ends of the country. The conversation went well; each was ready to find the other attractive, and it was exciting to play with possibilities in this way. The next step was to exchange letters, and Michael describes how 'Lucy wrote one and a half pages, very elegant and precise. I loved her writing and the way she expressed herself.' He laughs. 'I replied with thirty-six pages of drivel. I just poured it all out. She liked that, too, my spontaneity and openness.' By the time they were able to meet face to face, they were already well on the way to falling in love, and it would have taken a good deal of discouragement to stop the process. The first meeting more than fulfilled their expectations. They began a very passionate affair, and after a couple of months Michael moved to Lucy's home town.

We suffer from a kind of selective blindness when we fall in love, that leads us to ignore or dismiss any potential problems. As a client of mine who was newly in love said, 'It worries me that I can't think anything negative about her.' When the passion is running high, the need to experience union with the beloved is so strong that we will achieve it, somehow. It is as though, in recognising the god or the goddess in each other, we temporarily transcend the limits of personality. Our differences become something to admire, rather than a stumbling block. Thus Lucy enjoyed Michael's ability to flow with his feelings, while Michael loved her ability to condense, to analyse what she felt and express it clearly and economically.

Ironically, it was these differing qualities that led to their parting, about eighteen months later. As the first intensity of the love between them began to wane, they settled into partnership. What brought them to grief, as so often happens, was the way they handled conflict. After an argument, Lucy would want to talk about what had happened, to try to understand how they had got into difficulties, resolve any hurt feelings and learn from the experience. Michael's way of dealing with it, on the other hand, was to let go of the emotional tangle and move on, meeting each new situation afresh. Each began to be frustrated by the other's attitude. Lucy felt that Michael was avoiding the issues between them and trying to sweep any unpleasantness under the carpet. Michael felt that she was simply giving the conflict fresh energy, dwelling on events that were better lived and left behind, and not being open to what was happening in the present.

They could not find a way to resolve the problem. It became a huge issue between them, and what they had formerly admired in each other now became hateful. Michael saw Lucy as obsessive, neurotic, endlessly wanting to pick things to pieces and unable simply to be. Lucy was enraged by what she saw as his refusal to deal with trouble, avoiding responsibility and rejecting opportunities to deepen their intimacy. Slowly and painfully, they came to the point where they felt that they could no longer live together in love, and so they split up.

3

Their story tells us many things. It begins with what I often think must be the ultimate con-trick, the way in which romantic love alters our perceptions so that everything about the beloved is delightful to us – often to the amusement or dismay of our friends and family, who cannot borrow our rose-tinted spectacles. In the words of the poet, Robert Graves,

> *'Love is a universal migraine,*
> *A bright stain on the vision*
> *Blotting out reason.'*

Michael and Lucy were the same people at their parting as they had been when they met. Through the transcending power of love, they had moved into deep intimacy, and all the potential barriers to union had simply dissolved away. This state is no illusion. When we are in it, we can feel more intensely real and alive than ever before. But, as we know, it does not last. Sooner or later, we fall back into ourselves. If the tide of love has swept us into partnership, into living with another, perhaps having children or working together, then we have to learn how to engage on the everyday level as well, day by day, task by task, misunderstanding by misunderstanding.

Here is where relationship truly begins. Here is where we need to muster all the skills at our command, and start to learn new ones. We need to find support. We need to forgive each other, and ourselves, for being human.

Sometimes, of course, it becomes blindingly obvious, as the glamour drops away, that there is no chance of developing a part-nership. More often, however, the position is not so clear, as it was for Michael and Lucy. They chose to split up, but I believe that if they had wanted to, they could have found a way through. This is where support from others is so essential, so that when we get stuck in head-on confrontation, as they did, someone else is avail-able to offer a new perspective, another way of looking at things. There is always another way.

In saying this, I do not want to imply that it is necessarily always better to try to make the relationship work. Falling in love is, in many ways, an end in itself. We have the choice, then, whether to explore relationship or not. It offers us the opportunity; it opens a door that we might otherwise be too scared to open for ourselves.

What lies beyond that door is the subject of the rest of this book. For now, I should like to focus on what being in love means to us as individuals – not as a way of engaging with another person, but as an experience in itself. If we can disentangle ourselves from our preoccupation with the beloved, the state of being in love has some valuable insights to offer.

THE LOVE EXPERIENCE

For many of us, falling in love will be the most powerful emotional experience of our lives. To be in love is to step into an altered state of consciousness, an elevated place where we feel intensely alive, aware of our connections with the world around us, and full of wonder at its beauty. The barriers are down; through union with the beloved, we feel complete, no longer alone.

A person who is in love has moved the centre of their being so that it now lies between the lover and the beloved. The lover is in a state of ecstasy, a word whose root comes from the Greek *ex-stasis*, or 'standing outside oneself'.

Human beings have a deep need to experience ecstasy, and in the past we have most often found our way there in a spiritual or religious context. It is no accident that people often describe being in love in mystical or spiritual terms; thus, John Donne describes his mistress's bed as 'This love's hallowed temple.' It seems that as the place of ecstatic experience at the heart of spiritual life has been lost or suppressed, so its place in the realm of relationships – in romantic love – has become much more important to us. Our need to stand outside ourselves, to lose our separateness and to merge with the divine, will find expression somehow. If the path of spirit is denied to us, the need will find a way out wherever the walls of our personal castles are weak-

5

est. Hence, when we fall in love, we encounter the divine indirectly.

ROMANTIC LOVE: THE PEAK EXPERIENCE?

For all these reasons, we place enormous emphasis on falling in love. In the relationship stakes, this is seen as the peak experience, and for its sake we will justify huge upheavals in our lives; leaving established relationships, moving house or changing jobs, becoming estranged from parents and families. One client of mine left her husband and two young children, in secure financial circumstances, to live with a man who turned out to be frequently drunk and physically abusive. Even after she had more than once felt that her life was in danger, it was almost two years before she finally left him. When I asked her what it was that she saw in this man, she smiled wryly and said, 'He wrote poetry. I thought it was wonderful.'

The need to be with the beloved can be so strong that it overrides everything else. If we cannot or do not choose to submit to it, we suffer intensely. This path to ecstasy also makes us uniquely vulnerable in that our happiness becomes dependent on the actions and responses of another person. Alongside the bliss of being in love lies the torment of jealousy, the agony of not being loved in return, and the heartache of separation. If this is where we feel most alive, it is also where we may suffer the most intense pain.

This leads us back to the question of what romantic love really has to offer us. It is certainly not a way of ensuring that we live happily ever after, unless we are exceptionally lucky. Falling in love requires a temporary suspension of our critical faculties. The qualities that we see – or imagine we see – in another person, that lead us to fall in love with them, may be quite different from those needed to sustain a mature relationship. And, more often than not, what we are seeing has more to do with our own projections than with the reality of another human being. This is the next area that we need to explore.

'THE COURSE OF TRUE LOVE ...'

Consider a few of the particular circumstances in which we fall in love. For one thing, we do not tend to fall in love with people we already know well. There is a glamour about the beloved, a sense of mystery and potential, that does not sit well with old acquaintance. The mundane realities of their lives tend to get in the way of the love experience, rather than being an integral part of it, and this in itself might alert us – if we were not so deeply in love – to what is really going on.

Likewise, there is the apparent paradox that romantic love has a way of lasting longer if it is not consummated, or not returned: loving someone who cannot or will not return that love; loving without being sexual, in the way of old-fashioned courtship or the mediaeval tradition; or loving with limits of a different sort, as in a long-term affair in which the lovers choose, because of other commitments, not to live together. The ecstasy can be prolonged for many years or even for a lifetime, when it is not taken into full-blown, everyday relationship. Some of the greatest creative works have been produced by poets, writers, painters and so on, in such a state of grace.

What happens, on the other hand, when there are no barriers in the way, and we are free to explore our passion to its fullest extent? In my own experience, the state of being in love lasts for anything from six weeks to six months – perhaps longer, if there is some constraint, such as not meeting very often. After that, little by little, the glamour wears thin, and reality begins to show through. Our projections are brought home to roost; the goddess or the god departs. What then?

THROUGH THE LOOKING-GLASS ...

If romantic love is largely a process of projection, then it pays us to look at what we are projecting. What is it that we admire in the beloved, that we need to recognise or develop in ourselves? Much has been written about the way in which a man may project his inner feminine, or a woman her masculine, qualities onto a loved one, and what an excellent opportunity this can be to bring these parts of ourselves into consciousness. The process of projection, however, goes much further and deeper than that.

For we do not fall in love at random. In theory almost any two people can form a relationship, but we do not choose just anybody. Even when romance blossoms from nothing more than a moment of eye contact across a crowded room, we sense far more in that brief glimpse than we can possibly know. Neuro-Linguistic Programming, a highly sophisticated modern therapeutic technique, teaches that 93 per cent of communication takes place without words. Did you ever have the feeling, as you gazed into the eyes of your beloved, that somehow you had known this person all your life? At one level, this is nothing more nor less than the truth. We choose those who mirror us, those who will show us what we may be or become. All projections, however, have some anchor in the reality of the Other. Hidden within the beautiful flower of love and passion, the unconditional adoration that blooms in the first stages of romantic love, is the recognition of all sorts of other qualities in the loved one, some of which are anything but adorable.

As we move through relationship, and particularly if we explore intimacy with several partners along the way, we cannot help noticing that patterns emerge; the same issues come up time and time again, even when the new beloved seems, at first, to be completely different from the one before. For the work of relationship is spiritual work, and until we take up the challenge of self-transformation, it will continue to present itself to us.

The story which follows is an excellent illustration of all this, and it shows what can be learned, in the therapeutic context, from being in love.

PAUL'S STORY: UNREQUITED LOVE

In his mid-thirties, Paul had been exploring personal growth for two or three years, and in the last few months he had fallen in love. The problem was that he had fallen in love with a woman who was already in a relationship, and she had made it clear that that was where she wanted to stay. As relationship was out of the question, Paul's energies were channelled into intense self-examination. He had a fair understanding of where his feelings were coming from, but it made no difference to the strength of his obsession – his own word – and so he brought it to therapy to try to gain some new insight.

We began by looking at what it was about Sophie that Paul found so powerfully attractive. She was certainly beautiful, and was putting out strong sexual messages that had, in the time Paul had known her, drawn a number of men into her orbit besides Paul himself. However, as Paul explored his feelings, it became clear that, for him, the sexual attraction was not the primary factor.

What had really moved him was his sense of Sophie's vulnerability. 'She's well defended, but she's very vulnerable inside, and she sometimes has trouble making decisions or knowing what she really feels, and that really hooks me. I just want to hold her and protect her. It melts me inside.' Paul needed no prompting to recognise that he was responding to something of his own here, but he was finding it difficult to call the projection home. His own vulnerability was irritating to him, a source of shame, and he readily admitted that this had been his parents' attitude towards his insecurities as a young child. 'It's really hard to take that part of me seriously, or even to give it a voice at all. I tend to discount it automatically.'

This is a key point about projections, and one that explains much of their power. It is those parts of ourselves that we automatically discount, that we do not even give a voice to, that tend to emerge in this form. So it comes about, at least in Western culture, that women often admire men who manifest power in some way: the ability to achieve things in the world, to be single-minded, to 'be somebody'. And men, in turn, are attracted by softness, vulnerability, fragility – precisely those qualities which Paul saw in Sophie. We may laugh at these stereotypes when we recognise them, but they still influence our actions. As long as girls learn that it is not acceptable for them to be too powerful, and as long as boys learn that they must not show – or even feel – their feelings, we will continue to look to each other to do these things for us.

There is not even an equal balance here, for we live in a patriarchal society which values the qualities it sees as 'masculine' above those it sees as 'feminine', and so prizes achievement (on its terms) far more than knowing one's own heart. Hence, girls also learn that, although feeling is the province of the feminine, it is essentially weak, something to be ashamed of. They also learn to hide, even from themselves. And so we are all touched when we find vulnerability in others; we are all attracted to people who seem more vividly alive than we are ourselves. Our drama and our literature are largely concerned with the exploration of emotions – pain and joy intensely felt and lived – at a safe distance from our everyday lives.

How can we begin to own these qualities in ourselves, and to live them in our lives, rather than requiring other people to carry them for us? It is not enough, as Paul discovered, to understand what we are doing. Paul knew all about how projection works, and had been trying to apply this knowledge to himself, but it had made not a scrap of difference to the strength of his feelings. Understanding is fine as far as it goes, but the power of love arises in a different dimension of our being, one that is not in the least impressed by reason and analysis. In order to bring home these lost or potential parts of ourselves, we have to allow ourselves to experience them, to care for them, to bestow love where it rightfully belongs. In Paul's case, he had to allow *himself* to be vulnerable.

As we worked together, it became plain that it was no accident that he had fallen in love at this time and in this way. He had been working intensely on himself for some time, and he was now ready to reclaim his own vulnerability. He saw it as belonging to a much younger self, unsure and 'very childish, really', and at first it was hard for him to take it seriously.

Before he could really allow himself to hear the voice of his own younger self, he needed to focus on his feelings towards Sophie, and to gain some clarity about them. I asked Paul to put himself in Sophie's position, and to speak as though he were Sophie addressing Paul. Immediately, without stopping to think, Paul-as-Sophie responded with, 'It feels as though you want to own me.' This came with the force of true insight. As I watched him, I saw the change; his eyes lit up and his presence – there is no other way to describe it – grew stronger.

And once he was able to *experience* what was true for him, in his heart and in his body, rather than trying to think his way into it, a shift became possible.

When he tried speaking to his own younger self again, the difference was immediately obvious. The impatience and embarrassment he had felt earlier was gone, and in its place was a new tenderness, and a readiness to listen. 'I can see it's really hard for you,' he said. 'I haven't given you much space, and I don't always hear you very well, but I'll give it a go.'

For Paul, this was a first step in beginning to allow this and other unexpressed parts of his personality their rightful place in his life, and so to live his potential more fully. I would predict that as he continued to work on this – and it might feel like work, to start with – his obsession with Sophie would begin to fade. In nourishing the part of himself that called to him so strongly, he would no longer need to project it onto the outer world, and his love could be bestowed where it was truly needed.

The message for all of us is plain. If we can learn to bring home our projections and give them the attention they deserve, we will both be better able to look after ourselves, and we will be more available for real relationships.

How Do We Form Real Relationships?

We have looked at what falling in love has to offer us as individuals, quite apart from the possibility of relationship. We have seen how it nourishes us spiritually, and how it offers us the opportunity to know ourselves better, through the recognition of our own projections. Once we can see them and own them, we can begin the work of filling in our own gaps, living more of our potential, rather than looking for someone else to do it for us.

It is at this point that we begin to be capable of real relationship. When the enchantment of romantic love is at its height, it may feel as though we have found our soulmate, our 'other half', but this is an illusion. We cannot even see the other person through the dazzle. Relating only becomes possible when the spell wears off. And when it does wear off, we have some profound choices to make.

Now we stand face to face with another human being. A stranger, someone with needs and expectations of their own, which may or may not dovetail with ours. Someone equally bewildered, disappointed, or angry that we are not what we seemed to be. It is nobody's fault, but blame hangs in the air. The old defences spring back into place, sharpened by dismay that we have made ourselves so vulnerable, revealed so much. Maybe we have made promises to this person, sacrificed people or things that we hold dear. What do we do now?

The possibilities that lie ahead are only limited by our own fears and conditioning. We can leave, say goodbye. It was wonderful for a while, but we weren't right for each other after all; maybe next time will be better. There is grief and hurt in this, especially when one partner still wants to make a relationship, but it is as clear-cut as relationship ever gets, and it leaves us free to fall in love again. Like the other roads to ecstasy, love can be addictive. The myth is very persuasive; if love departs, it must mean that this was the wrong person after all. Somewhere out there, the ideal partner is still waiting ...

Or we can stay physically and leave emotionally, to a greater or lesser degree, hoping – though usually this is not consciously thought through – to cause the minimum of pain and disruption, meeting some of our relationship needs and denying the rest. Most of us have tried this at some stage. If the other person agrees to play the game, the foundations may be laid for a long-term, stable partnership. If you don't engage emotionally, you don't rock the boat. Many a marriage works like this, with large areas of compromise, and a tacit understanding that tricky areas will be avoided.

Most of us inherit this sort of model from our parents. In times when marriages were harder to dissolve than they are now, it was seen as something to aim for, a way of relating well. When we first fall into relationship, this and other models spring into action automatically. It is only by becoming conscious of what we do that we can open up the possibility of doing something else. Relationships tend to work on several levels at once, with different – and often conflicting – models operating in different areas. We chart an erratic course between our own projections and expectations, what we were taught and what we have learned, comfortable habits and the urge to change and develop. Occasionally, we catch glimpses of each other.

And at the other end of the spectrum of possibilities is the longing that seemed to be fulfilled by falling in love in the first place; to find true partnership, true meeting, an intimacy that leaves no room for compromise. Is such a thing possible? I believe that it is, and I also believe that falling in love offers us a glimpse of what may be. It is the ultimate con-trick, part of the divine plan to lure us into relationship. How else would we ever be persuaded, in cold blood and in our right minds, to let down our defences for long enough to engage with anybody else on such an intimate level?

But if it is indeed a con-trick, it is also much more than that. On the spiritual level, the ecstatic experience of being in love feeds us and brings us to life. On the mental and emotional level, it offers us an incomparable opportunity to wake up to ourselves.

DIVINE MADNESS

This may sound like a complete dismissal of romance as a worthwhile way of engaging with other people. It isn't. As something of a love addict myself, it has been part of my journey to look long and hard at what was actually going on for me, and to penetrate beyond the unrealistic expectations I started out with. At the same time, I celebrate falling in love as one of the most wonderful and blissful experiences available to us. If it is madness, it is divine madness.

We structure our lives so rigidly these days that, if we are not careful, the dangerous forces of passion and free creativity can get squeezed out, denied any place in the plan. The price we pay is that they become far more dangerous, far more likely to erupt without warning and wreak havoc in our orderly existence. However, if instead we start from the premise that these forces are at the very centre of our aliveness, and that the needs of the spirit are just as important as the body's need for food and drink, then the whole picture is turned around. Falling in love can be seen as the fire of the spirit burning more brightly, and we can honour it as it deserves, without necessarily investing too much in the possibility of relationship with the beloved. In the best sense of the word, it is a self-centred experience.

When we truly recognise this, we gain the power of choice. It is up to us what we do with it. We might choose to enter into relationship, or we might choose to consider, as Paul did, what we may learn from being in love. It could be that there is a part of ourselves that is seeking expression, as he discovered. It could be that we have not allowed enough space for spiritual ecstasy in our lives, and that it is finding another way to break through. And, beyond all the attempts to find meaning, we can simply choose to enjoy and rejoice in this wonderful gift that has come to us.

A Doorway To Divinity

Falling in love, like any other manifestation of spirit in our lives, remains essentially a mystery. It is something that eludes our best attempts to analyse it, and this is as it should be. The greatest truths can only be lived, not understood. What we can bring to the experience of falling in love, what transforms it from an unconscious acting out which may or may not lead on to relationship and new growth, is our awareness and our commitment to truth.

And beyond all this, there is the willingness to be open to spirit, to let go of control and be swept away, to revel in the gift of ecstasy and communion with the divine. That part of being in love is not something that anyone has ever regretted, and that is the part that we truly long for. When we recognise this, we free ourselves from the need to control what happens between ourselves and the beloved, and we can open ourselves more fully to our own aliveness.

Paradoxically, when we do that, we also open ourselves to the possibility of aliveness in relationship. When both partners own their own potential, their own divinity, then they are truly ready to recognise and to honour the god or goddess in the other. This is where relationship really takes off; not in the romance at the start, but growing slowly through the patient work of unpicking and rebuilding. If we do our work well, the rewards may be beyond our dreams.

2

Relationship:
The Lover's Journey

'For one human being to love another, that is the ultimate, the last test and proof, the work for which all other work is but a preparation.'

RAINER MARIA RILKE

'I don't know why anyone bothers with relationships. I've been hurt so many times. It's much easier just to be on my own and look after myself.'

These words were spoken in a group that I ran a few years ago. Jim, the speaker, was in his mid-thirties, and had been alone for eight years. He seemed, at first, content with the life he had made for himself, but just below the surface lay pain, seething anger and frustration, and complete bewilderment at the way relationships had let him down again and again.

WHY ARE RELATIONSHIPS SO HARD?

Why are intimate relationships so difficult? What happens to the intense delight and passion that we feel at the beginning of a new relationship, and why does this so often degenerate into chaos and bitterness, or a state of compromise that leaves both partners half alive? Is it wiser to give up on the whole enterprise, like Jim, and deal with our loneliness as best we can? If we had tried and failed so many times with any other project we set our minds to, from driving a car to learning to read and

16

write, we would have given up long ago. Looked at rationally, it makes no sense.

Relating, however, does not have much to do with reason. The force that drives us to keep trying arises in the heart, not in the head. Its roots are in the rich, dark soil of our emotions, and its expression in our lives is often inarticulate, raw, not open to understanding and analysis except through slow and careful work. I have supported many thousands of people as they struggle with this work, and try to make some sense out of the emotional tangles they get into. In my own life, I struggle continually with the demands and challenges of intimate relationship. Out of all this has grown the understanding that we emerge from childhood, as a rule, very poorly equipped to engage with each other in a meaningful and emotionally nourishing way.

The art of relating well is something that we have to discover for ourselves. Intellectually we can appear mature and wise, but emotionally most of us never grow up – and, if we do, maturity comes in our forties and fifties rather than at eighteen or twenty-one. We reach it, if we reach it at all, slowly, haphazardly, and with many mistakes.

Much of my work is focussed on the exploration and development of this art. What is good relationship? How can we get better at it? If our motivation for change comes from getting it wrong – as of course it usually does – then what does getting it right look like? Alongside the work of dealing with crisis, stagnation, loneliness, and all the other ways in which relationship can come to grief, there is the need to search for new and healthier ways of relating.

WHAT IS THE POINT OF RELATIONSHIP?

As we work to create good relationships with our lovers, children, friends, family and workmates, so we learn more about ourselves. When the ways of relating that we were taught by our 'elders and betters' – themselves adrift in a rapidly changing world – don't work any more, we have the chance to replace them with ways that do work, ways that reflect who we really are, rather than who somebody else thinks we should be.

Our explorations into relationship with other people can open us up to parts of ourselves that are dormant or stunted. As we saw in Chapter 1, the people to whom we relate, even superficially, hold up mirrors to us; mirrors in which, if we have sufficient courage, humility and the desire to grow, we may catch glimpses of who we really are. Perhaps you keep getting involved with people who are angry. What does that say about you? It may be that you are not expressing your own anger, and so they are doing it for you; or perhaps you have something to learn about coping with anger. Either way, there is an opportunity here to become more conscious of who you are.

And, as we become more conscious of who we are, what drives us to behave as we do and feel what we feel, so we begin to open up the possibility of change. We can move to a place where we are no longer at the mercy of events, of other people and of our own unconscious patterns. The range of choices available to us increases, as we move to a position where we are not victims, but creators. Life in general becomes a lot more fun, as we no longer need to spend our vital energy holding on to ways of being that do not serve us well.

Have you ever thought about how much vital energy it takes to hide your vulnerability, to suppress your anger, to keep up the 'nice guy' facade? Don't you sometimes long just to feel whatever it is you are feeling in the moment? I can share that with my partner, Amanda, and I can promise you that it is worth all the heartache, all the hurt on both sides, to come through to a place where we can simply be human together. That doesn't mean, of course, that we have stopped hurting ourselves and each other, or that our feelings and needs are always in harmony. What kind of inhuman relationship would that be? What it does mean is that we have changed, and are changing, some of the ways of behaving that did not work for us. It means that we try to stay open to each other, to be with our feelings – whatever they are – and to listen for the messages that lie beneath the temporary outbursts of madness. We have developed structures that hold our relationship, that are still standing when the storms have passed.

There is no such thing as a perfect relationship. There is no ideal partner waiting out there somewhere. There are only people – men and women. Some may be easier to relate to than others, but we are all carrying baggage, and we could all do with a helping hand from time to time. In order to be able to relate, we all have to learn how to make changes in ourselves and in the way we do things. So the first step – not just in relationship, but in all areas of our lives – is to understand what changing actually means, and how to go about it.

THREE STEPS TOWARDS CHANGE

Before we can begin to replace bad habits with good ones – to put it very simply – we have to go through the process of bringing them, as fully as we can, out of the shadows where they have their beginnings and into the light of day. As long as we remain unconscious of what drives us to behave as we do, we have no choice but to repeat the old patterns. It is not enough to say 'Next time will be different.'

I had a client recently who came to me after his partner left him, because, as he admitted, 'I wasn't able to support her when she needed it.' Charles is a management executive in his early forties, and he had always been very clear that he wanted 'a strong woman.' 'In the past,' he explained, 'when I've glimpsed the needy side of my current partner, I've always run.' This had now happened enough times for him to recognise the pattern. He truly wanted the next time to be different, but he did not yet understand what it was that he was doing, or not doing, to create his situation. We shall look more closely at Charles' story below.

Between the desire to change, and the reality of actually changing, there are three steps we need to take. They will appear again and again in this book for, whatever the problem may be, the same process must be followed on the way to transformation. The three steps are: noticing what we are doing; becoming aware of the choices that we have; and forming an intention for the future.

1. Noticing

Until we begin to notice how we go about things, we cannot change them. 'How?' is a more useful question than 'why?' at this stage. Finding reasons for our behaviour is important, and we all have a deep need to find meaning in what we do, but understanding why we act in a particular way does not necessarily help to change it. Noticing means focussing on where things go wrong, and becoming aware of what exactly is going on for us at that point. The help of loving friends, a counsellor or a therapist is essential; we cannot see our own blind spots.

For instance, if we look at the example of Charles, the first step is to be specific. I asked him to recall, in detail, an incident in which his ex-partner Jane had asked – directly or indirectly – for support, and he had failed to give it. What happened between them? What did they say to each other, and how was he feeling at each point?

Then I suggested that he imagine that Jane was present, and tell her what was going on for him. He also switched roles, speaking for Jane as he imagined she would be feeling. What began to emerge was that Charles could not bear to acknowledge his own neediness. He was a self-made businessman, with the deeply held conviction that to be needy or vulnerable was to be weak. He had managed until now by denying that he had a needy side at all, but the price he paid was that he could not handle need in his partners either. He had always felt compelled to end his relationships as soon as the issue arose, and so they never really got off the ground; until Jane, whose armour in some ways was even stronger than his, turned the tables on him.

It hurt; and with the hurt came the beginning of change. Charles was forced to admit to himself that he was vulnerable and needy, and that vulnerability and strength are not mutually exclusive. In fact, vulnerability and true strength go hand in hand. He had mistaken armouring for strength – as we often do – and he now began to learn that only by knowing, and honouring, our own vulnerability can we become truly strong. At the same time, he began to understand that if he had a needy side, then so would his partner. It seemed to me that the next time could indeed be different.

Out of this kind of close focussing, insights arise. When someone is in distress, it is hard for them to see clearly. Pain casts a blanket of fog, obscuring the true shape of things, and when we are in pain we try to find ways of avoiding it, which takes us further away from awareness. But if, instead, we stay with the pain, the picture begins to change. A landscape begins to emerge, and there will be landmarks that we recognise, signs that we have been this way before. Noticing, and doing whatever we need to do to honour the feelings that we uncover, enables us to trace paths through the wilderness, and begin to make sense of our lives. Once we know what it is that we feel, and what it is that we do, we gain the power to choose.

2. Making choices

There are always more choices than we think. As children, we model ourselves on the adults around us. We cannot help doing this but, in the process, we shut out an infinite number of other possible ways of being. We become imprinted with just a few tried and tested ways of acting and reacting. Then, when we encounter a new situation, when we attempt intimacy with someone whose conditioning is very different, we get stuck.

Often, I have worked with couples who have run into an impasse like this, where the only option left seems to be to separate, and so step out of the situation altogether, even though there may still be love between them. A good example is that of Bill and Sarah, who had been living together for three years when I met them. Sarah wanted to leave Bill because, although they still cared deeply for each other, she had come to feel stifled and powerless in the relationship. Not wanting to hurt him by leaving, she felt trapped, slid into depression, and was unable to see a way out that would suit them both.

Eventually Sarah decided that, for her own sake, she had to

leave. With that decision, she regained her aliveness and her power and, as the depression lifted, all sorts of new possibilities began to open up. She had never even considered the possibility of living alone before, but now she saw that she could leave and still stay in the relationship. More than that, living apart allowed the relationship to grow, and so Bill, as well as Sarah, found that his needs were met more fully. I am not, of course, suggesting that this solution would work for everybody; just that for Bill and Sarah, it was a creative way out of what looked like a hopeless situation.

We cannot change the other person in the partnership. Nor does it help to apportion blame. What we can do is to become aware of what drives us (step one), and then consider our options. Awareness opens up our vision, and gives us a wider perspective. From a higher vantage point, all sorts of new possibilities can be seen. And, as in the first step, other people – especially the partner with whom the 'problem' has arisen – can help us to open up to these possibilities.

The next step is to consider our options, and to allow ourselves the space to be creative, even to play a little. Doing things differently feels strange, and it takes time to get used to it. Trying out new ways of behaving in less emotionally loaded areas can help. If you are normally careful with money, for instance, you could allow yourself some outrageous extravagance; or, if money slips through your fingers, allow yourself to notice where it goes, and keep an exact account for a month or so. How does it feel to break the rules? Sidestep the usual routine, practise lateral thinking. Flexibility in one area of life, if we bring awareness to it, has a way of spreading into other areas as well.

3. Forming intentions

Once we have noticed what we do or what we feel, and thus freed ourselves to look at the choices available, we are ready to take the next step, in full awareness and taking full responsibility for ourselves. This means formulating our intentions as clearly as we can, and committing ourselves to bringing them into reality.

Again, it helps to be specific. Simply saying 'I intend to become a better human being' is not much use to anybody. Change happens little by little, with occasional dramatic breakthroughs, and it is on the level of the particular, the small scale, that we can attain it. Also, positive intentions are better than negative ones: 'I will not lose my temper with the children' is far less useful than 'I will play a game with the children for half an hour on three evenings a week,' for example – and even that may be asking too much. The commitments we make must be achievable, or else we simply set ourselves up for another fall.

Here, too, friends can act as supporters and loving witnesses, reminding us of our intentions and encouraging us along the way. The idea is to make it as difficult as possible to slip back into the old habits, so any device you can think of to help you achieve this is worth a try.

One client of mine, a young man who was studying computer programming, had come near to breaking point. He lived with his wife and children in a small house, and the room in which he worked was next to the room where the children played. The noise they made, just by doing what children do, made it impossible for him to concentrate, and he was constantly losing his temper with them. His rage frightened him, and so did the realisation that he was in danger of losing his family altogether.

There was not enough space in the house to move further away. Somehow, everyone's needs had to be met in a way that did not lead to conflict. After much discussion, with me and with his partner, he decided to change tack completely. Instead of trying to avoid the children, and getting angry about them playing, he resolved to *play with them* between 6 and 6.30 every evening. His partner would then give them their supper – a little later than usual – and put them to bed, which gave him two hours or so of uninterrupted study. It also created the space to give the children some positive attention; and, once they were party to the plan, they helped to make sure that his new intentions were carried out.

There will be many examples of these three steps in later chapters, as we look at how change can come about in various aspects of our lives. As well as learning how to make changes, we need to become conscious of the qualities we must develop to sustain good relationship. It doesn't just happen automatically, but we may have to get hurt a few times before we can begin to appreciate this. It is when we start to ask ourselves questions like 'Where did I go wrong?'; 'What happened to the magic between us?'; or 'How could he/she do this to me?', that we have the chance to examine and improve our relationship skills.

At the heart of this book lies the idea that there is a set of key skills that are needed to make relationship work. Some we learn from our parents and peers but, along with the useful conditioning which we may gain in childhood, comes a great deal that either gets in the way or is actively destructive to mature relationship. It is one of the challenges of adulthood to sort through this mixed legacy, consciously adopting what is good as our own, setting aside whatever does not serve us well, and finding new ways of relating that work better.

FROM PAST TO PRESENT

There is an urgency about this work that is unique to our times. The world has changed, almost beyond recognition, within the lifetimes of our parents and grandparents. The structures they grew up with have fallen away. The expectations and guidelines that they – consciously and unconsciously – handed on to us do not match our reality, and we have to find new ones for ourselves.

Consider just a few of the major changes that have occurred in the last hundred years. We can expect to live much longer, and in better health, than ever before, so that our growing time has been extended. In terms of intimate relationships, marriage for life might once have meant thirty or forty years at most; now it could mean sixty or more. Where are the role models for this kind of relationship? In any case, although people do still get married, more than a third of marriages end in divorce or separation – and, of those that do not actually break up, a large proportion are less than nourishing to both partners. People no longer expect to stay together 'for better or worse'. Divorce is easier than it used to be, and it no longer carries such a strong social and religious stigma.

Likewise, the shame that used to darken the lives of children born to unmarried mothers has been left behind, and their rights in law are the same as those of 'legitimate' offspring. More women nowadays earn enough money to live on, and this, together with the safety net of state support, means that women can – and increasingly do – bring up their children alone; they can choose to leave unhappy or abusive relationships from which there was formerly no escape. Women's legal rights have changed enormously within this century, from the right to vote, and the right to retain their own property within marriage, to the right to accuse husbands of rape. Reliable contraception for the last forty years has meant that, for the first time, women can control their own fertility.

All of these factors – many of which we now take for granted – have had the effect of dissolving much of the glue that used to hold relationships together. So what do we have left?

According to the models we have inherited, the proper place for intimate relationship is marriage, or at least lifelong partnership. Marriage used to provide a framework for the disposal of property, the rearing of children in a shared household, and a clear division of labour – the man, typically, working to earn money, and the woman looking after the home and the children. It was expected that the married couple would have exclusive rights in each other's sexuality – at least officially – and that they would look to each other for companionship and emotional intimacy.

Nowadays, however, it is quite unusual to find all these factors within the framework of a marriage or partnership, although some of them may be. More people live alone, or with new partners, and the children live with one parent or the other. Women are no longer expected to stay at home with the children unless they choose to do so.

Choice is the key. Our parents – and particularly our grandparents – did not have, or did not allow themselves, this freedom to choose. Marriage was for life. What this meant, in terms of the quality of relationship, was the understanding that, since the external forms of partnership must be preserved, its emotional and spiritual sides had to come second.

Freda is a client in her seventies, who now lives in a nursing home. She is bright, aware and intelligent. Her husband, Eric, died six years ago, and her story is that her marriage was a long and happy one. Some time ago, during one of our sessions together, she talked of waking up feeling very sad and tearful, but being unable to cry. When I asked what stopped her, she recoiled a little, and then said, 'I haven't been able to cry since I was a child. When I was with Eric and I felt tearful, he used to pat me gently on the shoulder, and say, "Please don't do that, dear".'

Other factors that emerged in the course of therapy made it clear that this was indeed a happy relationship, because both parties accepted without question that the husband was the lord and master. If one partner always calls the shots, and the other agrees to that, of course there will be no conflict – and absence of overt conflict is one of the traditional ways of judging the success of a relationship. Without conflict, it is unlikely that there will be much room to grow, but personal growth did not come very high on the traditional agenda.

Emotional wellbeing, in fact, was something of a hit-or-miss affair, and the guidelines for emotional behaviour then, as now, were passed on by example. Whatever our elders *said* we should do, what they actually taught us was to do as they did. We learn by absorption, long before we are old enough to consciously under-stand what we learn, and it is these lessons that go deepest.

What we learned from our elders, what worked for them within the limits that existed at the time, was the art of compromise. Arguments, and the expression of anger in general, were unpleas-ant, and to be avoided if at all possible. Therefore, areas of conflict were simply not dealt with; or one partner gave way, swallowed his or her feelings and had to deal with them in various indirect ways. A couple learns, by trial and error, what flows easily between them, and what is dangerous ground. If conflict is to be avoided, the dangerous ground must be fenced off, and we must venture only where it is safe to go.

THE COST OF COMPROMISE

The trouble is that swallowed feelings do not simply disappear; try as we may to deny them, reason them out of existence or find some safe way of dealing with them, they have a habit of leaking out somehow. The 'safest' course is to turn them inward, onto oneself, where they manifest as physical or emotional illness, or loss of energy.

Doctors' surgeries are full of people on tranquillisers or other medications, trying to deal with symptoms like these. Linda is a typical example. She is twenty-nine years old, and she got married at nineteen in order to escape from what she described as a sterile home life. She first came to see me after having been treated with Prozac (an anti-depressant) for a few months. When she returned to the doctor for a fresh prescription, he wisely refused, and sent her to me instead.

She appeared strikingly attractive, energetic and open – in fact, not at all depressed. What really struck me was that she was immobilised by the conflict within her. This was how she described the situation:

> Colin is a really nice man – good with the children, kind and generous. When I married him, he was twenty-one years old and already middle-aged. I didn't know any better then, and I was happy for the first eight years. We have three lovely children, a nice car and enough money to live on. I feel so ungrateful, but this relationship is smothering me. I enjoy going out, being with people and having fun. Colin just wants to put his feet up at the end of the day and, although he never says it in so many words, I constantly sense his disapproval of me. He does say I've changed, and not necessarily for the better.

Linda's 'depression' arose, as it so often does, because she perceived her situation as hopeless. In her relationship with Colin there was no room for expansion, no space for aliveness, excitement or passion. Like many of us, Colin seemed to have buried his own need for these things so deeply that he was not even aware of his loss, and Linda's increasing desperation only made him feel confused and threatened.

Linda herself began by saying that she was confused but, as I listened to her, it became obvious that she was not confused at all. In her heart, she knew exactly what was going on. This sort of 'confusion' arises when there is conflict about what is real. Linda's upbringing had led her to believe that her life contained all the ingredients for happiness. Her husband, her family – and, to start with, her doctor as well – supported this view, which meant that there must be something wrong with her. There was no one in her life to whom she could talk without being judged in some way, until she was sent to me.

My task was simply to listen, to help her sift through the layers of pain and guilt and desperation and hopelessness, until her own wisdom, the wisdom that none of her family wanted to hear, could emerge. Here, there was no confusion. Linda knew that, unless she could find nourishment for her spirit within her marriage, it would simply starve. She would become truly depressed, dependent on tranquillisers to deaden her pain and help her bear the burden of her life.

We explored the possibility of change within the marriage. What was Colin prepared to do to keep it alive? The answer was, not enough. He continued to deny that there was anything wrong, and he could not understand what Linda was trying to say to him. For a relationship to grow, there must be willingness on both sides. Linda was faced with an agonising choice: to stay, and try to cut herself down to size, or to end the marriage. In fact, as I sensed quite early on, she had made her choice some time ago. All she needed was the permission to know her own heart, and the courage to act on that knowledge.

Eventually, after a couple of short separations, and much heartache on all sides, she left. It has taken her a year to come to terms with her decision and begin to find a direction for herself but, in her own words, the decision was 'the best choice I've ever made.' Linda's predicament is typical of the kind of struggle facing women in our times, as they realise that they don't have to sell their souls any longer in order to fit into a restrictive and suffocating mould.

Besides taking tranquillisers or becoming physically ill, there are plenty of other indirect ways of handling emotional pain or lack of fulfilment. Some of them 'work', in the world's terms, better than others. Pouring all one's energy into work is an obvious example. Others are less acceptable, or less easy to justify, though no less common: drinking, eating disorders, becoming depressed, having affairs. The cost of avoiding emotional engagement is higher for some than for others, but there is one price that we all have to pay, and that is in terms of aliveness. Each time we draw back from potential conflict, each time we choose silence or conciliation rather than expressing what is true for us, we die a little.

And yet, here is the central paradox. We enter into relationship in the first place because it is one of the main places in which we find our aliveness. We are social creatures; we exist in a web of relatedness, to ourselves, to the people around us, to other sentient beings, to the world we live in, and to the divine, whatever our concept of that may be.

We cannot live without relationship and, within that, we crave intimacy. We find our greatest aliveness, we feel most fulfilled, when we engage most closely with others: when we are in love; when we make love; when we create something with another person – a child, a piece of work, a shared experience. We find it, in fact, when we venture onto the dangerous ground where conflict may arise.

So we are left with an unprecedented challenge, one for which there are no role models and no paths to follow. The old structures that held our parents' relationships together are not as binding as they used to be. We can never return to their world, even if we regret the passing of some of its qualities. These days we are free to enter into relationship for its own sake, if we choose to do so – and most of us do make that choice.

I know plenty of people who are not in intimate relationships right now, but very few of them want to stay that way for the rest of their lives. We need intimacy, and our need is constantly at odds with our fear of being hurt or betrayed. The old models are no help; in fact, they are worse than useless to our attempts to relate to each other honestly, for they do not match the way that we actually are. It is up to us to develop new relationship skills for the new territory that we are entering. In the next chapter, we shall begin to look at these skills.

3

Laying the
Foundations of
Relationship

'And let there be no purpose in friendship save the deepening of the spirit.'

KHALIL GIBRAN, *The Prophet*

In an ideal world, perhaps, we would acquire the right skills before entering into relationship – rather like training for a career. In real life, however, we have no choice but to pick up our training as we go along, trying to build strong foundations for a house in which we are already living. If we do not choose to do this, it may collapse, and we will be left either with no relationship, or with the empty shell of one.

What are these strong foundations? In this chapter we shall look at some of the most basic relationship skills, and how we can learn to use them. Fortunately, we are all blessed with the ability to learn new skills. We can start to recognise what works for us, and what gets in the way of intimacy. Not all of what we learned in childhood has to be thrown away, and some of us have less unhelpful baggage to carry than others. Nor are the skills that we need truly new – 'under-developed' is perhaps a better way of describing them.

These key skills, or building blocks of good relationship, have emerged from my work over the years, as I see the same issues coming up for clients again and again. Some are very simple, and relatively easy to learn or to get better at. Others are more difficult, requiring a greater degree of self knowledge and emotional maturity.

KEY SKILLS IN RELATIONSHIP

The first three skills are about learning to listen, learning the language of the Other, and learning to appreciate. At one level they are very straightforward but, once we start to practise them in the obvious ways, other avenues of communication begin to open up, and these can have profound and dramatic effects on the quality of our relationships.

1. The art of listening

In a conversation between two people, what usually happens is that while one is talking, the other is filtering what he or she hears, interpreting, making judgments, and getting ready to reply as soon as the first person stops talking. Effectively, we take it in turns to talk about our own experiences or observations.

In a discussion about something 'out there', an exchange of ideas and information, this works fairly well. If the subject is feelings, however, it won't even take you to first base.

When we are trying to express our feelings – and this is an art in itself, of which more later – we need to be heard without judgment, without interpretation, and without our experience immediately being capped by that of the other person, especially if the other person is a partner, a lover, or someone equally close to us. To put it very simply, we need to be *received*.

This need to be received, to be heard, is a very basic one, and it is one of the things that moves us to seek relationship in the first place. We know when we have been truly received, when someone has really listened or 'been there' for us: we grow quiet inside; our hunger is satisfied. And if we are not heard, we remain restless, unappeased.

Young children demonstrate this very clearly, before they learn how to hide or suppress what they feel. When we ignore them, give them partial attention or try to reason or shame them out of their feelings, they simply try harder. As soon as they feel heard, it is finished, and they go on to the next thing. Children are good people with whom to practise the art of listening.

What stops us from listening to each other? Essentially, it comes down to fear. Fear that we will not be heard ourselves, that if one partner is heard then the other cannot be (this is a very common dynamic in couple relationships). Fear that the feelings of the other person will hurt or damage us in some way, so we must put up our defences before they even begin to speak. And fear, underneath it all, of the very thing that we long for: true meeting, open and vulnerable and unguarded. What might happen then?

In that place of true meeting, we risk being truly naked with one another – and in our nakedness we are defenceless. We can be deeply wounded or almost destroyed. How can we ever dare to take such a risk? Actually, we have no choice, if we wish to find the ecstasy which we know is our birthright. We can put off making the choice for a thousand seemingly valid reasons; we can go on marking time until the end of our days. But why waste this precious gift of life and passion? We can go beyond safety into love – and, paradoxically, here is where true safety lies. It is the harbour in which we long to rest.

The only way to develop the art of listening is to do it. Like a lot of skills, it improves with practice. In the groups I run, we use a very basic exercise in listening, in which two people sit together and take it in turns to talk about themselves. While one speaks for five minutes, the other listens, not interrupting or commenting or giving any feedback; just listening with the best attention they can muster. Listening is not passive – it is both active and receptive. For the listener, it is an exercise in learning simply to be present. It is easier to do this with someone new, with whom you have no history, than with someone close to you, but it is still surprisingly hard.

In the day-to-day flow of life, of course, we never stop to listen to each other in a structured way like this, but there are plenty of other ways in which to practise the art. The very process of building a relationship, for instance, requires us to learn the language of the Other. The same words can carry a very different meaning depending upon how they are spoken, and by whom.

2. Learning the language of the Other

Relationships can all too easily come to grief because the two people involved simply do not understand each other's language. I have worked with many couples who are locked in bitter conflict, each desperately trying to make the other hear, and completely missing, or misinterpreting, what is being said to them.

A good example is that of Nick and Judith, with whom I worked over a period of three years or so, from the time when he left her and their three children in a state of acute crisis, through a long separation during which they could hardly talk to each other outside their therapy sessions, to a time when they could once again live together and take their partnership forward into uncharted territory. They were in their mid-thirties when I met them, both intelligent, articulate, and intensely miserable together.

Nick was a quick-tempered man, like his father. His response when things did not work out as he wanted them to, or when he felt hurt, or under pressure, was to fly into a rage. He was never physically violent to Judith or to the children, but he would shout, bang doors and sometimes storm out of the house. Beneath the rage, as he slowly came to understand, was a terror of being abandoned, of losing everything. He associated this with a time in early childhood when he was seriously ill and, according to the practice of the time, was taken away from his family and placed in isolation in hospital for several weeks. On a more everyday level, he also felt that his mother had not 'been there' for him emotionally.

Judith, on the other hand, was unable to see any of this. She found his anger terrifying. Her response was to freeze, to retreat inside herself where she could not be reached. She could not say what it was that she feared but, as we worked together, it began to emerge that her own father had beaten his children when they annoyed him. He had also been sexually abusive. The survival strategy that she had adopted as a child had been to disappear as completely as she could.

Quite unconsciously, she was still doing this. At the merest hint of a threat she would shut down, becoming totally unavailable emotionally. This, of course, would incite Nick to further rage, and so a dreadful vicious circle had developed. Neither of them, as so often happens, could talk about it to their friends, who saw them as having a very good marriage, and were shocked when it suddenly fell apart.

On the surface, it appeared that Nick was the aggressor and Judith the victim. At a deeper level, however, they were not really interacting at all. Instead, each was using the defence tactic that he or she had learned long ago. Nick's defence was rage, and Judith's was withdrawal. Both tactics have a dual purpose, in that they hide the users' real feelings, not only from others but from themselves as well. So these two people, who so desperately needed to be heard, had found a very neat way to perpetuate their childhood patterns. As Judith herself said, 'We got married because our neuroses were compatible.'

For Nick and Judith, the deadlock only ended when his leaving propelled them into therapy. In their sessions together, because a third person was present to hold the space for them and to act as both witness and interpreter, they began in time to get beyond the opening words of their familiar emotional dialogue. They began, in fact, to understand each other's language.

And, once they learned to listen for the underlying messages, those messages began to get clearer, the defences less automatic. Judith came to realise that, although she still felt afraid of Nick's anger, she had a choice as to how to deal with it. If she withdrew when he became angry, as she had always done, nothing would change. But if she stood her ground and did not disappear, something different would emerge.

They began to have real arguments, as she found her way to her own feelings of anger. The child in her felt that standing her ground would invite some unspeakable retribution. Instead, as

Nick felt himself to be met and heard, not only in his rage but in what lay beneath, his desperation began to subside. And, as he could see and hear Judith more clearly, it became less possible to react to her as he had learned to react to his mother. They could meet, sometimes, as adults. As adults, they could reveal their own pain and vulnerability, and offer each other support. Out of the wreckage of their marriage, a mature relationship began to grow.

So, listening can lead to some dramatic changes. When you listen skilfully you begin to notice. From the simple, everyday level of noticing when your partner is upset or tired or wanting to celebrate, it opens the door to deeper levels, and gives permission for the unheard parts of yourself to find expression. As we have seen, noticing is the first step in becoming conscious. And once we are conscious of our patterns of behaviour, we have the opportunity to change them.

Listen quietly, and with an open heart, and what you hear may not be what you expect. What have you got to lose?

3. The art of appreciation

This, again, on a mundane level, is laughably simple but seriously under-practised. It means noticing when something about your partner – or anybody else, for that matter – pleases you, and saying so. How often do you notice that he or she is looking good, has taken time and trouble over some household task, or been there for you in some way? When you do notice, how do you acknowledge it?

It is all too easy to take each other for granted, as we once took our parents for granted. Letting each other know that we are valued and appreciated is fundamental to the success of relationship, and so often we simply forget or do not bother to do it. This does not mean being artificial or finding things to praise all the time. Rather, it means expanding and giving attention to the part of us that does value and appreciate.

Once again, there is much more to this than appears on the surface. What happens when somebody pays you a compliment? We have plenty of ways to discount compliments, of course, but, even if we do that, we are warmed a little. Our self-esteem gets a boost. Everyone likes to be appreciated; very few of us could not use a little more admiration. It draws us out, we allow ourselves to expand and be more expressive. And when people express themselves more, not to impress others or to take power in some way, but from a place where they feel truly good about themselves, they become more beautiful.

We learn, from an early age, to take on board what people say about us. If you receive praise for your efforts, admiration for your beauty, and encouragement to explore your potential – as is the right of every child – you will believe that you are a praiseworthy and admirable person with much to offer in relationship, work and creativity. Your self-esteem will be high, and your life will be full and rich. Most of us do not receive such wholehearted affirmation, and we believe there are parts of ourselves that are not lovable or admirable in any way. We need help from our partners and those around us to get in touch with our own beauty.

I shall say more about self-esteem in the next chapter, for it is the cornerstone of good relationship. The point I want to make here is that appreciation is self-fulfilling. If you treat your partner like dirt, then that is what you will have to live with. And if you treat your partner like a goddess or a god, for even a tiny fraction of the time you spend together, you will be making space for something wonderful to emerge.

CREATING SUPPORT

As well as developing these key skills within relationship, we have to learn how to build and maintain support outside it. No one person can meet all our needs, yet so often we try to load all our demands on to a single partner who must be our sexual, emotional and spiritual companion to the exclusion of all others. Then, when we run into trouble with this relationship (as we almost certainly do) who else do we have to talk to? And what happens when we are not part of a couple at all?

Creating support is fundamental to the building of a strong relationship, and yet it is a skill that is desperately under-valued and under-developed. We cannot possibly hope to sustain a living, growing, intimate partnership with one other person, unless we also have strong connections outside and around that partnership. Over-dependence on one exclusive relationship is encouraged in our culture, with its horror of showing emotions in public and its exalted ideal of romantic love. But the plain truth is that nothing is more likely to bring about the death of true love than to overload it in this way.

Support can come from many directions, and the more of them we can draw upon, the better. Each has its strengths and its weaknesses, and sometimes one will be more appropriate than another. The main sources of such support are our families, our friends, support groups, and professional counsellors or therapists. There are other resources, such as books or solitary meditation, that we can explore on our own, but in the end there is no substitute for the warmth of human contact.

Support in the family

If you have maintained close ties with your parents or brothers and sisters, this may be the first place you go when you are in distress.

But beware. Even the most wise and loving parents find it hard to allow their children to be in pain. It is hard for them to suspend judgment, not to blame, when they see you going through agonies with your chosen partner. They cannot help taking sides; and, although this may be balm to your wounds at times, it may not always benefit the relationship. Their first concern is your survival and wellbeing, not the survival of your partnership. That means that it will be up to you to decide, step by step, whether their support is appropriate or not.

And for the majority of us, whose parents are less than perfectly wise and loving, the pitfalls are far deeper. When we first encounter difficulties with a partner, we come up against two barriers: our own immaturity, and the limitations of the role models our parents have provided. In other words, if part of the problem lies in what we learned from our parents, we cannot look to them for help. We have to find new role models, and helpers with wider vision.

So families are a resource to be used with caution and awareness. In order to find the kind of support we need on our journey into adult relationship, we must look further afield.

Support from friends

The next obvious source of help in times of trouble is our friends. These are people with whom we have chosen to develop a connection, usually because of some experience or interest in common.

However, these connections may not work for us when it comes to opening up, showing emotional distress, being vulnerable. There is such a conspiracy of coping in our culture, such pressure not to show that we are in trouble, that very often we have to come to the point of complete breakdown before we can let the 'brave face' slip. I have counselled so many people who, although they may be surrounded by friends with whom they share work or play, do not feel that there is anybody with whom they can share pain, or talk honestly about what is closest to their hearts. Very often, we do not even have the language with which to speak about these things, and this is yet another new skill to learn.

Anna is in her late fifties; a warm, wise, passionate and outgoing woman who is surrounded by friends and acquaintances. She has weathered many storms in her life, and she struck me at first as someone who had built up a very well-developed support system and knew how to use it. Recently, however, her resources had been stretched to their limit. Her mother, who was very emotionally demanding, had become too frail to live on her own any longer, and had gone to live in a home. Anna saw that, instead of sustaining her, the home was killing her; she hated it so much that she wanted to die. In her compassion, Anna had her house redesigned so that her mother could come to live there. All her friends told her she was crazy but she could not bear to let her mother suffer; however, their relationship was very intense and demanding, and having her mother in her home proved to be every bit as difficult as her friends had feared.

She thought she had sufficient support from her partner, but here her own words revealed the problem – 'He's incredibly patient and understanding, but I just can't keep taking from him. It's not fair.'

When I asked whether there were other friends to whom she could talk, she answered at once, 'Oh yes, lots!' I pressed her to be more specific; who, exactly, could she go to? This time the reply was more hesitant; 'Well, there are a few . . .' What emerged was that Anna, with her open heart and ready compassion, tended to be the one to whom others came with their troubles, and this one-sidedness had become a habit. Fortunately, once she realised this, she also saw that there were ways of redressing the balance, and so she chose two friends with whom she could begin to do this.

When we do try to opt out of the conspiracy, and find friends with whom it is possible to acknowledge our real feelings, it very quickly becomes clear who is willing to take this journey with us, and who is not. We have all experienced how, when we make changes or go through crises in our lives, some friendships lose their vitality while others endure. In fact, a crisis is often the very thing that opens the door to deeper intimacy with a friend and, although you may dread the thought of admitting that your life seems to be falling apart, the response you get may surprise you. Consider how you would feel if someone you cared for let down their defences and showed you their need for a good friend. Would you feel put upon, or honoured? In the same way, if you are honest with yourself, you will know which of your friends would be honoured to receive your confidence.

In order to build a strong and flexible support system, it is necessary to discriminate. Once again, it is a question of noticing what goes on when you are with your friend, and making a conscious decision whether to invest your energy in this friendship, or not. Ask yourself, how does this serve me? Do I feel energised after spending time with this friend, or am I drained? Do we support each other in our growing, or do we have an investment in staying as we are? When I am in pain, do I have to hide it, or will I be lovingly received?

If we are to grow and flourish, we need to surround ourselves with a like-minded community, one that will honour creative self-ishness in its members, celebrate playfulness and self-expression, and accept us for who we are. Friends who are committed to the journey of self-fulfilment will be learning, as we are, how to care for themselves, to feel their own feelings, and to find paths through the maze of intimacy. In my own life, my close friends provide me with communion of spirit and emotional nourishment. I trust them to give loving support when I need it, and to challenge me when I need that too.

One of the side-effects of improving your self-esteem is that you become unwilling to settle for anything less in your friends; and if old friends won't or can't welcome a relationship rooted in truth and fearless integrity, then perhaps it is time to find some who will.

I have talked about friends in the plural, and mentioned the concept of *satsang*, or the community of like-minded people. This is very important, for one friend is not enough. As a therapist, I often meet people who have no intimate friends at all, but just as often a client will say, 'Oh, but I do have one friend I can really talk to.' One is better than none, but one still won't always meet our needs. What happens when your dearest friend is away, or immersed in troubles of her own?

Carol was a client of mine who recently came close to suicide when her friend suddenly broke off all contact. Carol was going through a long depression, and had been phoning her friend several times a day. Quite simply, the good will ran out. If we put all our eggs in one basket, this risk is very real. And even when the load is not so great, there will be uncomfortable places in any one friendship, mutual blind spots, unspoken contracts, that limit its potential as a tool for expansion and experimentation with new ways. Friends, like intimate partners, can also come to support each other in not growing.

How can we create a network of friends that will both support us in our partner relationships and enable us to meet the needs that one partner alone cannot fulfil? It may happen of its own accord but, just as we cannot expect the 'right' partner to magically appear in our lives one day, so it is unlikely that good friends will simply manifest themselves without any effort on our part – though sometimes they do.

And yet, it is also unnecessary to go looking for them. The places where they are to be found are places most of us need to visit in the course of our journey. As part of our self-unfolding, we may explore in many directions. If your need at the moment is to develop your potential for painting or dancing, or creative writing, for example, the obvious thing to do is to find a class or a group which focusses on this activity. There, you will find other people who are engaged in the same process of discovering themselves, and who are just as much in need of support as you are. Together, we can travel much further and faster than we can on our own.

Support from therapeutic groups

A therapy group provides a wonderful source of people committed to personal development, ready to act as witnesses, play roles, give support, and challenge where you are holding back. I love the richness and fertility of the group environment, the space that it offers to try out new ways of being, with people who have no stake in the old ways. It is a superb place to begin repatterning your relationships, to take risks and make mistakes, and see what happens when you really allow yourself to be vulnerable.

A lot of what goes on in the groups that I run is not strictly therapy at all. Recently, I held an ongoing group that ran for six weeks, one evening a week. At the first session there was the usual mixture of people, all bringing different issues and life experiences, including one woman who had never done any sort of therapeutic work before, and who was understandably very nervous.

During the evening we each talked a little about what we hoped to get from the group, and then we danced together. Later, we listened while another woman spoke about her conflicting feelings as she tried to support her husband through a serious and potentially fatal illness. It was clear that she was in great need of sup-

port herself, and afterwards she lay down, with soft music playing, and the rest of us gathered round to give what we could
through the loving touch of our hands. She cried a little, and some
of us cried with her. Finally, we closed the evening by holding
hands and chanting.

Afterwards, the newcomer remarked in wonder, 'I didn't think
therapy was like this!' It isn't. Much of the work of therapy is
hard, painful, stripping away illusions and confronting old
wounds and fears. It demands stamina, strength, resilience, the
willingness to face unpleasant truths.

And yet, what is therapy? For me it is also about opening our
hearts to each other, crying and laughing together, witnessing each
other's pain and finding that there is healing in the act of witnessing.

And there is more; it is also about being joyful, being expressive, being passionate, being silly. Within the group, there is the
opportunity to try out some of these neglected skills, too. 'Shit-
shovelling', as a client once described it, is an essential part of the
work, but it is also about turning shit into compost, a rich source
of nourishment for the potential self that is beginning to unfold.

This work, as a rule, is a gradual process. A weekend group
won't change your life, and any that claim to do so should be
avoided. What it may do is to move you, sometimes profoundly,
and great things may come of that; but be careful. To get the most
from a short group, you should have a good support structure
already in place – good friends, a therapist, co-counselling, for
example – which will help you to integrate and build on any shifts
that may happen. Real change means practising a new way of
operating, again and again, until it becomes established. This
doesn't happen overnight, nor in a few days – but it need not take
years, either.

I find that longer-running groups work best of all, because the
bonding that happens between the group members becomes a
powerful support structure in itself, a new 'family' in the best
sense of the word. During the lifetime of a year-long group, for
instance, 'work' done during a group meeting can be taken into
everyday life and practised, and the changes that are set in motion
can be brought back to the group at the next session. As well as

being a crucible for transformation, the group gives its members the support that enables them to ground their transformations in reality.

Support from counselling and therapy

One-to-one work is quite distinct from group therapy and, although they overlap a great deal, seeing a counsellor or therapist can answer different needs and bring out different responses. As a therapist, I see myself as a kind of midwife of the psyche, witnessing and supporting my clients as they give birth to themselves anew.

The therapeutic relationship is different from all our other relationships. It is also unique in history, a tool devised specifically to help us find our way through uncharted territory. A therapist is not a priest or a healer, not a friend or a relative, though the relationship that is created may take on qualities that we recognise from other contexts.

What we ask of a therapist is that he or she hold no vested interest in the way we are, no judgments or preconceptions that will keep us from finding out what is true for us. During therapy time, for one hour a week or whatever the contract may be, we ask that this other person be present for us, giving us total attention and unconditional acceptance. And, to the extent that the therapist is able to be present in this way, healing can happen. So much of the pain that we carry comes from not being heard, not being seen, not being allowed to be who we are, that this in itself is profoundly transformative. It is so rare, in everyday life, to be truly present with another person for more than a few seconds at a time, that many of us have to begin simply by learning what it feels like.

Most people come into therapy in a state of crisis. Life is not working; problems are insurmountable. You get into the same messes again and again, driving round and round the same roundabout, unable to find the exit. Simply admitting that you can't do it on your own, that you need a helping hand, is the start of the process. Once begun, it takes its own course; you can use therapy as pain relief, a place to discharge tensions so that you can carry on with your life, or you can use it as an entry into self-transformation, and take that as far as you choose.

The core of the relationship, the soil in which growth can take place, is the quality of the therapist's attention. You will know whether he or she is truly there for you by whether you feel safe to explore the deeper and darker levels of yourself, the places you are too frightened to go into on your own. If the therapist is denying something in you, or judging it as unwholesome or ugly in some way, the process cannot continue. I repeat, you will know. If you feel blocked, check what is happening for your therapist; and if he or she is not open to being challenged, it may be time to move on. We are in the business here of repatterning, of building healthy and honest relationships; and in this one relationship, if nowhere else, you owe it to yourself not to settle for anything less.

The therapist's ability to accompany you on your journey springs from his or her own self-development and self-acceptance. I cannot be with a client in places I am not willing to go into for myself. I cannot be present with compassion, without judgment, unless I remember my own humanity. I cannot allow my client to reclaim his or her power, to rejoice as the magic and wonder of being alive are restored, if I am not comfortable with my own power, my own magic. And unless, at the end of the day, I can acknowledge the client as an equal, the therapeutic relationship will stop short of maturity.

❦❦

THE NEXT STEP: COMING BACK TO OURSELVES

In this chapter, we have begun to look at some of the basic building blocks of relationship, and at the kind of support structures we need if we are to succeed in our building. Before we go on to consider further relationship skills, it is time to turn inward, and to focus on a particular skill, without which our attempts to relate to others will be seriously handicapped from the outset. In order to seriously begin the work of loving another, we first have to learn to love ourselves.

4

Self-Esteem: Learning to Love Ourselves

'The love for my own self is inseparably connected with the love for any other human being.'

ERICH FROMM

Good self-esteem is the rock upon which relationship is built. Your capacity to love another – not need, but truly love – is only as great as your capacity to love yourself. And so, if you want to learn to relate with passion and aliveness and without fear, you must start by putting your own house in order.

What does it means to love ourselves? How do we lose our self-esteem, and how do we go about rebuilding it?

FALLING FROM GRACE

We are born beautiful. How do we judge that something or someone is beautiful? By our own response – the wonder or pleasure or heart-catching tenderness that beauty evokes in us. Babies and children evoke that response, in those of us not too deadened by our own pain to feel it; it is their birthright. Their beauty lies not only in their physical appearance, but in their joy and vitality, the way they express themselves without self-consciousness, their vulnerability. And we love these qualities in

46

adults too, when we catch the occasional glimpse of them. But by the time we reach adulthood, most of us are so hedged about with inhibitions, self-doubt and self-dislike that these glimpses are all too rare. So what happens in between?

We have children for all sorts of reasons, and – knowingly or not – we load upon them all sorts of dreams and projections. Some are personal: 'Be what I never managed to be'; 'Follow in your father's footsteps'; 'Love me unconditionally', and so on. Others are cultural, and are often taken for granted: 'Don't show your feelings', for example, is something that most English people take on board, but it is by no means common to the rest of the human race.

As the child grows, and his or her uniqueness becomes more obvious, conflict arises. We cannot be all that our parents want us to be, however hard we try. And with that realisation comes the first blow to our self-esteem: 'If my mother doesn't find me beautiful just the way I am, then I am not beautiful. In order to be beautiful, I have to change. I have to become less noisy/more obedient/eat what I'm given/be polite to people I don't like ...' The list goes on, and there are endless variations on the theme, but the message the child gleans is the same: 'I am not all right as I am.'

It does not matter how gentle or enlightened the parents are, or how carefully they try to foster the child's spirit. None of us reaches adulthood without some damage to our self-esteem, and it is part of the work of adulthood to reclaim it. The process of socialisation makes us smaller. We are receiving messages all the time, firstly from our parents and other caretakers, and later from siblings, friends, teachers and the wider world around us: messages that say, whether subtly or directly, 'This is okay. That is not okay.' And so we cut ourselves down to size, we close down parts of ourselves that do not meet with approval, and we grow up to be functioning adults, utilising a tiny part of the potential that we were born with.

The price we pay for conformity is simple and dramatic. *As you stop being yourself, you stop liking yourself.* The more you sacrifice your truth, the less love you feel for yourself, even though your mother or your classmates or whoever are assuring you that you are far more lovable when you behave as they want you to behave. And with self-love goes ease of self-expression, the capacity for joy, the ability to make mistakes, to take in and let go.

An interesting example is that of Nigel, who came to one of my year-long training groups. Nigel appeared to suffer from what might be called a 'superiority complex'; rather than having low self-esteem, he seemed to feel that other people, on the whole, were not good enough for him. He came from a wealthy family and had inherited a great deal of money, together with a beautiful house and land. Despite his good connections and material advantages, however, he was not happy. His relationships with women had always been short-term, because sooner or later his partner would fail to live up to his expectations. Friendships were also a disaster, for similar reasons.

Committing himself to a long-term therapy group took great courage for Nigel. It was not long before he found himself challenged on all sides for, to the other group members, he appeared arrogant, aloof, lacking in feeling for others and unwilling to give of himself. There were times when I thought he would leave the group, but his armour was so strong that challenges simply seemed to bounce off, leaving him unmoved. It was several months before he began, slowly and painfully, to open up.

What emerged was that, from babyhood onward, a strong sense of his own importance had been instilled into him. He was special, he was different – but not because of any intrinsic quality in himself. His importance, his worth as a human being, lay in the fact that a great deal of family wealth and property would eventually be his. Almost daily, it seemed, his father had alluded to this in some way, and impressed upon him that this placed him above other people.

Nigel had inherited this belief along with his wealth, but the other side of the legacy, of which he himself was only half aware, was a total lack of appreciation of himself, Nigel, simply for being who he was. He had never been seen, let alone loved or valued, just as himself. How could he possibly even begin to know what was missing? And, of course, most of the people he met in the course of his life had also been blinded by his status, and had been unable to see beyond it – or had not cared enough to try. In the group, however, Nigel was forced, again and again, to witness the pain of others and to stay with their bewilderment and anger as they bruised themselves against his defences. Eventually his own pain became too great, and the defences began to slip. Behind them, behind the mask of Nigel the inheritor, was a lonely, frightened, desperate little boy who had no idea how to go about the business of loving and being loved, let alone any sense that he deserved it.

Here is where the alchemy of group support begins to work. As the other group members began to be able to see his pain, his anger, and also the delightful child that he had once been, so they began to warm towards him. Nigel began to experience real liking from others, for the first time in his adult life. As he allowed it in, his defences softened further.

By the end of the year, when the group broke up, he had made four or five friends with whom he stayed in contact. They were able to support him in beginning to dismantle some of the self-destructive behaviour patterns that he had built up in order to deaden his pain, and which eloquently expressed his lack of love for himself. The most urgent of these was his heavy and habitual drinking, which had grown from being a natural part of his lifestyle to an addiction. He could not break it on his own, and with no strong and loving relationships in his life, he had had no reason to do so. Now, however, instead of helping him to cope, it began to get in the way. Through receiving love from others, Nigel began to be able to love himself, and to want to care for himself better.

THE COST OF LOW SELF-ESTEEM

When it comes to making relationships, low self-esteem is an enormous handicap. We make poor choices, we give up too easily or refuse to let go, and we sabotage the flow of love in all sorts of ways, if only to give ourselves the sour satisfaction of proving, once again, that we're just not worth it. People tend to gravitate towards others whose self-esteem is at a similar level so that, on the whole, we get exactly what we think we deserve. A relationship between someone with high self-esteem and someone with low self-esteem is unlikely to survive, if indeed it ever gets off the ground in the first place. As a friend of mine put it, 'I went looking for a goddess, but when I found her, she was looking for a god.'

Of course, there are plenty of ways in which we try to convince ourselves and other people that we're really just fine, thank you. We wear masks most of the time; masks that we've learned, one way or another, will get us approval or liking or some kind of positive attention. Some are designed to achieve the opposite effect, to make us less noticeable. The masks say to the world: 'This is who I am. I am a nice person. I care for others. I make people laugh. I am a success in my work. I am attractive, sexy, dynamic. Please, look no further.' As my friend and fellow therapist Leo Rutherford is fond of saying, 'I'm fine' really stands for 'I'm Fucked up, Insecure, Neurotic and Emotionally unstable'!

There's nothing wrong with masks – they are an essential part of our lives – but when we use them to deny the underlying reality, then we are in trouble. If we can never take them off, we can never really touch and be touched. I remember Jim, who came to one of my five-day groups and entertained us all with his razor-sharp wit. For the first three days I was delightfully amused by him. The mask was a work of art; it took me that long to see that his humour kept everyone at arm's length, and shielded him from his own feelings. Beneath it was a deep well of sadness and despair. It was only when the mask was removed, and he was able to allow himself to feel liked – and hence likeable – in this vulnerable state, that he began to see that he need not wear it all the time. The relief was incredible. We cannot appreciate, until we take our courage in both hands and unmask ourselves in this way, what an immense effort it is to keep smiling, to maintain the charade.

Often, we can hide our self-hatred even from ourselves. It is hard work, desperately hard, to keep it all together and convince yourself and the rest of the world that you're okay, you're making it as a human being, if behind the bright facade is the secret knowledge of your own worthlessness, but it can be done. Millions of us do it every day.

It works quite well, though the cost is high, until something comes along that is outside our control, something that breaks down our carefully built structures and lets in the forces of chaos. Losing a job, ending a relationship, having a quarrel with a friend, even just the washing machine breaking down – it only depends on the thickness of our veneer. Someone with a healthy self-regard would rage or grieve at such an event, and then muster their resources to meet the situation. But someone with low self-esteem is suddenly immobilised, stopped in their tracks by the uprush of despair and self-loathing, the voice that says, 'I'm no good. There's no point in anything.'

How Not To Get Help

Peter was a member of an ongoing monthly group. He worked as a counsellor, and had cast himself in a largely supportive role. He tended to be perceived by others as strong, solid, gentle and trustworthy. He was often the last to speak, and usually had little or nothing to say, yet this clearly stemmed from difficulty in expressing himself rather than from a state of peace and serenity.

At our eighth meeting, it was obvious that he was in some distress, though he tried not to let it show. When someone asked what was the matter, he tried very hard to turn the attention away from himself, saying that he did not want to stop other people from having a good time. This is one of the tricks we can use to stop ourselves from getting help in climbing out of the pit of despair; we imagine that we will somehow infect others with our own darkness. In fact, as Peter found, those close to us cannot help being aware of it at some level, and it affects them insidiously, indirectly. Far from being a burden, it is usually a huge relief to them as well as to us to bring it out into the open.

Peter's next argument was that it would be more painful for him to talk about, or express, his feelings than it was to keep them under wraps. Not surprisingly, this did not cut much ice with the group. Once you have broken through this barrier for yourself, and experienced the sense of lightness and new energy that it brings, this particular defence begins to lose its power.

He also feared that 'If I allow myself to open up in the group, then I only have to go back into the outside world, and it will be worse then because I'll be feeling, and I won't have the support.' This fear is partly justified, in that, once we begin to allow ourselves to feel, it becomes much harder to close down again. However, the answer, rather than keeping the lid firmly shut and once again refusing to honour our own needs, is to set up the support we need in the 'outside world' as well. Groups are not separate from real life, and other group members are only a phone call away. To deny ourselves such support is yet another form of self-sabotage.

Faced with the refusal of the group to leave him alone with his misery, Peter was bewildered. What had he done to deserve so much loving attention? The answer, of course, was nothing. We do not have to do anything at all to deserve time and care from others – or from ourselves. This, for Peter, was the turning point. If all these people think I am worth bothering with, then maybe I am. When we truly cannot find it in us to love and care for ourselves, then the first step towards healing is to allow ourselves to receive love from other people.

Peter wept, a few difficult tears. For him at that point, this was a major step in self-exposure and trust. It takes time for us to digest new experiences; we have to allow enough space for them to become integrated into our lives. Sometimes change can be revolutionary, but more often it happens slowly, step by step, as we gain the courage to take small risks and challenge the habits of a lifetime.

At our next group meeting, Peter was the first to speak, rather than the last. He revealed more of himself as he spoke, and this in turn changed the responses of other group members. People felt him to be more trustworthy, simply because they could see him better. The caring, supportive stance which had been his refuge was not lost; instead, his relationships within the group took on a new vitality, as the possibility of both give and take began to emerge.

One change leads to another, making it progressively harder for us to hold on to our old patterns. With hindsight, of course, the rewards that follow this kind of risk-taking far outweigh our fears of ridicule or rejection, but the first step is always the hardest. The fear is real. A kind of death awaits us, the death of the persona with which we have faced the world, and it is appropriate to be afraid.

THE DISCIPLINE OF SELF-LOVE

People often think that it is somehow self-indulgent to look after themselves. On the contrary, it demands practice and discipline, and continued vigilance to make sure that the time, space and nourishment that we all deserve in our lives do not get squeezed out by the demands of work, home and those around us.

There's an element of self-discipline, too, in the task of rooting out negative feelings about ourselves. They don't serve us in any way. They get between us and our aliveness, our experience of our own beauty and that of other people; yet we cling to them, indulging ourselves in them. It is painful to be useless, stupid, ugly or whatever our particular putdown may be, but it is a safe, familiar pain. The process of regrowing ourselves is a slow one: seldom dramatic, often difficult and disruptive, as we outgrow the limitations that were all we thought we deserved.

Sometimes in my groups I conduct a ritual in which each person chooses to throw away some quality or way of behaving that does not serve them any longer. When therapy or willpower is not enough, magic will sometimes do the trick. It is a superb way of focussing our intentions, and declaring them before witnesses.

People choose all kinds of things to throw away – 'my inner critic', 'my anger with my ex-partner', 'my addiction to chocolate' are a few that have come up recently. But all our resolutions, in the end, stem from the knowledge that, through lack of care and love for ourselves, we become our own worst enemies, and that forming a clear intention to get rid of some of the useless baggage that weighs us down is one of the first steps to self-healing. Gestures like this can be extremely helpful in our efforts to transform our lives. They may need to be repeated many times, but each time a space is opened into which we may grow.

The work of change, then, begins with noticing what we do to sell ourselves short or put ourselves down, and recognising that, as adults, we create our own lives. Whatever we were taught as children, it could not possibly encompass the immense potential we each carry within us.

We have a choice: to stay within the boundaries we were given as children, or to take responsibility for ourselves and create our own. Paradoxically, those of us who have been most gravely hurt in childhood are those who are most likely to break free from the old limitations and to widen our choices for ourselves. Pain provides the impetus. Changes come about as a by-product of exploring the areas of damage and, as these inner changes begin to happen, so we become capable of choosing to make conscious changes in our outer lives as well.

RE-PARENTING OURSELVES

When we cannot care for ourselves enough, we look to others to do it for us. Usually unconsciously, we search for someone to be for us what our parents could not be: always there, always loving, never letting us down.

The bad news is that this search is doomed. Until we learn how to be mother and father to ourselves, the child within will continue to reach out to anyone who gets close enough. Sooner or later this child, with its desperate neediness, its unreasoning demands, and its inability to see anyone else's point of view, will be hurt again. And again. Before we can truly love and be loved by others, we have to learn to look after ourselves, to give ourselves what our parents could not or would not give us.

As we learn, as we begin to act from a place of strength rather than pain, so what we expect from relationship changes. When we look at those close to us – partners or friends or parents or children – we no longer see our own projections, but other human beings, able to meet us in some ways, and not so able in others. When arrows are fired at us, we begin to see that we do not have to be wounded, that the person wielding the weapon is acting from his or her own pain. Eventually, compassion grows. And when appreciation comes our way, we no longer side-step it like a matador dodging a charging bull. We allow it in; we accept it as our due.

SINGING OUR OWN PRAISES

I have several exercises that I often use in my groups, as part of the business of building self-esteem. One of them simply involves sitting down with two or three other people, and taking five minutes to tell them about all your good qualities, the things you like about yourself. Five minutes can feel like forever! We have strong inhibitions about 'blowing our own trumpets', and it can feel very dangerous – almost like courting retribution. The experience of being heard and accepted, even celebrated, in this way, is a revelation for many people.

In another exercise, which usually comes at the end of a group, each person in turn invites truthful feedback from the other members. This is a very powerful exercise. It is so rare, in day-to-day life, to see ourselves honestly reflected back by other people. It can be surprising, delightful, illuminating, and sometimes painful, but it is always a source of learning. Within the safe context of the therapy group, whatever comes out of it can be handled as necessary. And what does come out of it, despite people's fears, is nearly always overwhelmingly positive. Most of us are perceived by others in a far better light than we imagine.

In everyday life, we have all sorts of ways of avoiding or discounting or not hearing compliments, but within the group, with witnesses, we can choose to take a risk and let them in. In everyday life, too, when someone tells you that you are beautiful, for example, you can easily persuade yourself that their judgment is lousy, they've got ulterior motives, or they wouldn't think so if they *really* knew. But at the end of a group, in which you may have wept and raged and exposed your inner darkness, when two or three or more people tell you that you are beautiful, you might just begin to believe it.

LOVING OURSELVES ON FOUR LEVELS

The work of rebuilding and reclaiming goes on at many levels. For the sake of clarity, it is helpful to look at a human being in terms of four realms – the body, the emotions, the mind and the spirit – while recognising that all such distinctions are arbitrary, and that what is happening in one part of our being inevitably affects the other parts as well. We also need to be conscious of the hierarchy implicit in this view, in that we tend to regard the physical as the 'lowest' level and the spiritual as the 'highest', and do ourselves a grave injustice in the process. With these provisos in mind, we can begin to look at the way low self-esteem affects us at each of these levels, and how we can go about changing this.

1. Loving our bodies

On the first level, that of the body, our love or lack of love for ourselves is at its most visible. It is not hard to see when someone is not at ease in his or her body. The way they move, their clothes – too smart, or not smart enough – the way they speak and express themselves, all tell the story. And because we are taught to see the body as the lowest part of our being, it is an easy focus for self-hatred. We use and abuse it, ignoring the messages it gives about its true wants and needs. Eventually our health begins to suffer, in one way or another.

Here is an invitation to wake up and begin the work of healing; we can choose, either to try to suppress the symptoms and carry on along our chosen path, or to stop and take the time to ask ourselves, why is this happening? What can I do to change it? Suppressing or ignoring symptoms tends to lead to further breakdown, more loss of life force. We can, quite literally, allow ourselves to die through lack of self-love.

I am not suggesting that we are to blame for all our bodily ills (thinking in that way ends up as yet another form of self-punishment), simply that we owe it to ourselves to take responsibility for the way we are, and to take appropriate action. What that action may be depends, of course, on the individual, but its roots are to be found in the part of us that says, 'I am worth looking after. I deserve better than this.' The rest is down to good solid support, a measure of faith in results which may not be immediately obvious, and the discipline to keep noticing, keep coming back to the new path, until old self-destructive habits finally begin to loosen their hold. Anyone who has been through the process of dieting or giving up smoking will understand what this means.

Together with the other members of one of my long-term groups, I witnessed this process happening for Dorothy, a woman in her thirties. She had always been 'big', and she had built this into her persona, as people often do, so that it became linked with the qualities of warmth, generosity and openness – qualities she prized in herself. The dark side, the hidden price which is paid by so many women in our culture, with its rigid and – for most women – unattainable standards of beauty and attractiveness, was that she did not feel beautiful, or worthy of being loved by others. Certainly, she did not love herself as she was, and her secret shame about her body made her unable to meet other people on an equal footing.

Dorothy had been in therapy for some months and, as she began to open up some of the places where she had been wounded, to begin the work of healing and of looking after herself, so her self-esteem began to improve. One of the things she really began to enjoy was movement and dancing, as a way of expressing the new creativity and zest for life that was rising within her, but she was becoming increasingly frustrated with her body's inability to do what she wanted it to do. 'I really want to be able to move freely and lose myself in the dancing, but my body just won't let me,' she said. And so, witnessed by the group, she declared her intention to shed some of the weight she was carrying.

During the year, we kept company with Dorothy as she carried out her intention, changing lifelong habits, and dealing with the emotional revolutions as the fat began to disappear. By the time of our final meeting, she had lost about five stone, and she felt and looked completely different. Here was a woman who was proud of herself, who knew that she was worth looking after. The weight loss had happened – and this is a very important point, the key to understanding why so many diets fail – not as an end in itself, but as a by-product of her rising self-esteem. Rather than serving any purpose, her excess weight now got in the way. At our last meeting, Dorothy danced, ecstatically, beautifully. Watching her, watching the joy and vitality shining out through her dancing, I was moved to tears.

2. Loving our feelings

This leads on to the level of the emotions and of self-expression, for our ability to look after ourselves physically has its roots in our emotional state, most obviously when we use food, tobacco, alcohol and so forth as a direct means of suppressing our emotions and dulling our pain.

Lack of self-esteem shows up on the emotional level as a lack of *joie de vivre*, or basic zest for life. This leads on to depression, emotional greyness, and ultimately to despair. How do you feel when you wake up in the morning? Can you shout when you feel like it, cry your eyes out or laugh your head off? Can you play like a child, make mistakes and let them go? How do you express yourself creatively? Creativity is an essential part of being human, and a person who is not creative is suffering from the loss of self-love. It doesn't have to be painting or playing the piano or 'making' anything in the obvious sense, just some way in which what you do expresses something of your truth.

When I lived in London, I used to travel to work every day on the 74 bus. I always made a point of trying to catch the 8.45. The conductor was a middle-aged, genial, bearded chap, who created a magical environment on his bus. Each passenger was made to feel special, from little old ladies to po-faced businessmen. His sense of humour was electric, and never malicious. A sense of merriment pervaded the journey, and I always got off feeling recharged. In his ordinary way, that bus conductor was being extraordinarily creative, and touching many lives with brightness.

Once again, the road back to self-love involves noticing what we are doing, forming the intention to change it, and then bringing that intention into reality. As Dorothy found, it takes time, continued attention, and loving support. Making time and space to be creative can be hard, if your life is full of other, apparently more important commitments, but it must be done, for your life's sake. One step leads to another, and it is a process that becomes easier and faster as you begin to give yourself the message that you are worth it.

Here support, in the form of loving friends or possibly therapy, is vital. This work cannot be done alone. Low self-esteem flourishes in isolation, fed by the original wounding that cut us off from ourselves and from other people. The way back lies in speaking and being heard, expressing our 'negative' feelings and being received. The people around us provide mirrors that will show us how we are doing, whether we inspire love and affection, whether we are valued for our own uniqueness. Self-expression needs to be witnessed, and from self-love flows joy in the company of true friends.

3. Loving our minds

On the level of the mind, lack of self-esteem can manifest itself in various ways. A common result of wounding in childhood is for a person to become cynical and unable to show enthusiasm, with a tendency to put down other people in order to feel safe and in control. Or they may be cautious and tentative in their thinking, afraid to pursue ideas for fear of ridicule, and unable to believe that their ideas could have any value in any case. In an extreme case, someone who has been badly hurt may turn their rage and fear outward, looking for a relatively safe place to vent these feelings. This leads to intolerance, narrow-mindedness and bigotry; the root of prejudice is pain.

Another common way in which low self-esteem can show up is in mental 'cleverness', or intellect without heart. Cleverness is generally approved of in our culture, and it can enable us to attain some of the goals we are taught to strive for, such as money, success and power. Many of us are driven to try too hard intellectually, believing that, if only we can 'make it' in the eyes of the world, we will be all right. Unfortunately, the goalposts tend to keep moving and, however successful we may become, the starving child within remains as hungry as ever.

The same is true of those of us who retreat into the mind as a refuge from feeling, living in our heads and doing our best to deny our pain. The pain is still there, even if we cannot feel it, and the head is a poor place from which to conduct relationships.

I am reminded of Isabel, a woman in her forties who took part in a year-long group. Her insights were acute, but she used them like javelins, knowing just where to aim to hurt most. Hers was a clarity without kindness, a piercing vision, and people tended to avoid engaging with her, once they learned that they invariably came off worst in any encounter. She held power, certainly, and she commanded respect, but it was a lonely place to be.

Her position in the group accurately reflected the way she had set things up in the world 'outside', and it showed her very clearly how arid her emotional and spiritual life had become. What fuelled her mental sharpness was despair, born of pain carried for many years and never shared. Once she had taken up her position, and driven everyone off to a safe distance with her barbed comments, she could not reach out when she needed to, and break through the defences she had created.

During the long summer break, Isabel decided to go on a prolonged spiritual retreat. Here, in silence and solitude, backed up by guidance and support when she needed it, she found the nourishment and solace she was seeking.

When the group came together again in the autumn, we noticed an astonishing change in her. The quality of her presence was no less powerful, but in a very different way. She had become both stronger and softer, with a new humility that enabled her to offer her insights in such a way that they could be received gladly. Thus she, in turn, could receive what came to her from others.

Generally speaking, as Isabel came to understand, the way to look after our minds is to look first to our emotional and spiritual health. The intellect is fed by free creativity and by the openness and lively curiosity that follow from emotional wellbeing, and it is kept in balance by a strong connection with spirit.

On the practical, everyday level, we can be discriminating in what we choose to take in, whether through reading, films and television, theatre and so on, or through the company we keep. Again the question can be asked, does this nourish me? Do I need to read the newspapers if they simply feed my despair? Is it good for me to be with people whose thinking I find uncongenial? If we take the time to ask the question, the answer is usually clear, and then we can make a conscious choice, honouring ourselves in the process.

4. Loving our spirit

On the last level, that of the spirit, low self-esteem reduces our ability to touch and be touched. We lose the sense of something greater than ourselves; awe, wonder and reverence are removed from the spectrum of our feelings. How can you feel confident that you are part of the divine scheme of things, life's celebration of itself, if you are convinced that you are just not good enough?

For many of us, the pain of this exile from the realm of spirit is so great that we try to deal with it by denying the reality of the sacred altogether, and take refuge in the mind or in the myriad diversions that the world offers. There's a paradox here, in that it is pain – through crisis, grief, the loss of hope – that very often forces us to look beyond ourselves, to open up to spirit once again. When we recognise that we cannot cope on our own, then we have begun the work of healing. Isabel's story is a good example of this process at work.

The particular road that we take is not so important; what matters is whether it is a path with heart. Again, if you are part of a religious community or church, you can ask yourself, does this truly strengthen my connection with the divine? Is my soul nourished here? Can my fellow travellers be with me in my grief, my vulnerability, my celebration? Finding true spiritual community, or *satsang*, is a vital part of learning to love and care for ourselves. Without it, we cannot be whole.

Equally, some form of spiritual practice helps to recall us to ourselves when we lose the way, and keeps the channel open for the flow of joy and wonder in our lives. It need not be formal prayer or meditation; there are countless ways to commune with spirit, from being alone in nature to playing football. Whatever takes you out of yourself, brings you into the present moment, and leaves you feeling refreshed and at peace, is communion with the divine. Without some such communion, whether conscious or unconscious, our spirits starve. And when love for ourselves begins to grow, and flow between us and those around us, more and more of our lives are spent in this communion. Jesus said, 'Except ye become as little children, ye cannot enter the Kingdom of Heaven.' As we reclaim our birthright, we again become like the little children we once were, sure of our place in the world, re-entering the Kingdom of Heaven.

5

Expressing Emotions: The Heartland of Relationship

'To laugh is to risk appearing the fool.
To weep is to risk appearing sentimental.
To reach out is to risk involvement.
To expose feelings is to risk exposing your true self.
To place your ideas and dreams before the crowd is to risk
their love.
To love is to risk not being loved in return.
To live is to risk dying.
To hope is to risk despair.
To try is to risk failure.
But the greatest hazard in life is to risk nothing.
The one who risks nothing does nothing and has nothing –
and finally is nothing.
He may avoid sufferings and sorrow,
But he simply cannot learn, feel, change, grow or love.
Chained by his certitude, he is a slave; he has forfeited
freedom.
Only one who risks is free.'

ANON

We come now to the place where we fight our fiercest battles and attain our closest intimacy. For a relationship to work, for it to be nourishing for both partners, there must be a strong emotional meeting. This does not mean perfect harmony; in fact, quite the reverse. It means a willingness to be real with one another, to feel whatever we are feeling, and to deal with whatever responses there may be. If we can stay with that, then we have a chance of winning through to genuine closeness, true intimacy, a place that lies way beyond the apparent closeness of being in love.

Why is it so hard for us to do this? The answer is to be found both in the present and in the past. Ultimately, though, it is because we fear that if we show who we really are, we will be rejected, not received, not loved. If we want to be loved, we must never take off our masks.

THE PRESENT: HANDLING OUR EMOTIONS

Picture the scene in the early days of what you hope will become an intimate relationship. You are anxious to impress, to be seen in your best light. Already in love, or well on the way there, you are viewing your would-be lover through a golden glow, and automatically discounting his or her less-than-wonderful qualities. If something upsets or irritates you, you hold your tongue, not wanting to dispel the magic. And it works, for a while. But as the magic begins to seep away, these minor irritations start to grow in importance. Some of them may become major stumbling blocks. What happens next?

Here the road divides. If we have already learned something about expressing our emotions gracefully, and with respect for the other person, then we are well on the way to creating a viable partnership. If not, then the first real row may demolish the fragile structure that we have begun to build. Feelings that have been suppressed have a way of attaching themselves to something trivial – like the legendary toothpaste tube – and spilling out clumsily, wounding those whom we love, shocking us out of our fond illusions, and destroying trust, perhaps for ever. If we are used to hiding our feelings, then the next step, after conflict has arisen, is to try to hide our hurt as well. Not wanting to make ourselves vulnerable to this other person who has wounded us, we retreat; and so the distance between us grows.

Then there is the third way, the way of continued suppression. Partnerships where 'difficult' emotions are simply not handled can last a long time – perhaps a lifetime – although the cost is high in terms of aliveness. When we sacrifice the free flow of rage and tears, we also lose our joy and our passion. There is always the risk, too, that we will meet someone else who will call out these buried feelings – all the more intensely because they have been denied expression for too long.

The story of my client, Tom, illustrates this only too well. Tom had been married for nineteen years to Carrie, and together they had brought up three children. It was a good, solid, respectable marriage, and all seemed well. Then Tom became friendly with one of his wife's friends, Sarah, attracted by what he described as her 'craziness' and ability to enjoy life. They began a wild affair, and he discovered in himself an enormous sense of fun that had never found expression in his marriage. He left his wife, then tried to return, torn between his love for her and the children and his new sense of himself.

The return was a failure for, though Carrie too yearned for more fun in her life, somehow they could not rekindle the spark between them. He now lives with Sarah, and his children no longer speak to him. Some way further along the road, the same problems are beginning to crop up with Sarah that he encountered with Carrie, and they are not having fun any more. The message in this cautionary tale is a stark one: unless we learn to recognise what we feel, whether 'good' or 'bad', and to communicate it honestly, we are condemned to follow the same patterns again and again.

Where do these patterns come from? To answer this question, we need to look at how we take our first steps in learning to handle our emotions.

THE PAST: PARADISE LOST

Somewhere in early childhood, we begin to learn the art of hiding what we really feel. The emotions of a young child are strong, vivid and immediate. She cannot contain her grief, her joy, her rage; she cannot postpone it until a more convenient moment, or express just enough for those around her to cope with. But strong emotions evoke strong reactions, particularly in adults who have learned, in their turn, to push their feelings down. Usually, the so-called 'negative' feelings are the ones they have trouble with. Anger, fear and grief stand at the top of the list. Sexual expression takes its place here too. And there are other emotions, not usually labelled 'negative', which are often disapproved of, subtly or not so subtly: the expression of excitement, joy or enthusiasm, for instance. Each of us could make our own personal list.

The reactions of adults may vary from subtle disapproval to outright physical violence, but the message we get as children is the same: it is not all right to feel this way, or to show that we feel this way. And so we cut ourselves down to size, as best we can. And we survive.

What happens to the feelings we suppress? They don't just depart, never to darken our doors again. As long as we are alive – and this is a blessing, not a curse – there is something in our being which is continually striving for wholeness. They wait, just beyond the threshold. Sometimes they seep in, under the door or through the keyhole. When our attention is drawn that way, we hear them knocking for admittance. And sometimes, when we are in crisis or the effort of keeping it all in check simply becomes too great, they break down the door and erupt into our lives, causing chaos.

We are right to fear these unwanted guests, for they threaten the order that we work so hard to maintain. Suppression gives them more power; they grow stronger and darker, with far greater destructive potential than they ever had in the first place. People who come into therapy are often terrified of their own pent-up feelings, particularly their anger. They imagine that, if they give vent to their rage, they may destroy themselves or other people. There is no doubt that many acts of violence are fuelled by intense emotions, but I am pleased to say that, in my experience, nothing so catastrophic has ever happened in a therapeutic situation. Instead, the time bomb is defused, and the relief of finally giving up control is immense. The energy invested in suppression, and the power that these banished spectres hold, can return to where they rightfully belong.

The feelings that give us most trouble fall into four categories: fear, anger, grief and sexuality. Other emotions that often cause problems in relationships can be seen as variations on these themes: jealousy, for example, contains elements both of fear and of anger. I have also mentioned enthusiasm, joy and passion, but in my experience there is less need to work on these directly, for, as we feel our way back into our so-called 'negative' emotions, so we regain our ability to have and to express the more 'positive' ones as well. Each of these four types, if not felt or not expressed spontaneously as they arise, will colour our lives, and limit our ability to relate to others, in different ways. Sexuality is the province of Chapter 7; we shall explore the first three below.

FACING OUR FEARS

What do we do when we are afraid? At the simplest level, there are three kinds of response. Suppose, for instance, that you are suddenly faced with a dangerous wild animal (probably the most likely event that our fear responses originally evolved to cope with). You might scream and run for your life, and this would be an active expression of your terror. Or you might freeze, unable to move, which would be a passive response. The third way, if you were able to ride the fear and use the rush of adrenalin to help clear your thinking and speed up your reflexes, might be to find some unexpected strategy to save yourself – climbing a tree, perhaps, or throwing dirt in the monster's eyes.

All these possibilities have some survival value, depending on the circumstances, but it is obvious that being able to keep your head and not go into a blind panic would give you the best chance of escape. There are two points to be made here. One is that unless we are used to facing fear, working with it and seeing beyond it, we do not have that third option. We can only go with our instinctive gut reaction. The other is that the ability to 'keep your head' when you are afraid comes with experience and emotional maturity. Some adults can manage it some of the time, but a young child cannot do it at all.

Children find many things terrifying. As adults, our response varies according to whether we judge their fear to be appropriate or not. When it is appropriate, to our grown-up eyes – fear of a growling dog in the street, for instance – we are still likely to find some fault with the child's response. In the case of the dog, we would probably try to slip past at a respectful distance; but the child would be just as likely to scream its head off or become rooted to the pavement. The child's fear is then a problem for the adult to deal with. Even when the child suffers from night terrors, to which most adults tend to respond with sympathy – at least at first – we say things like 'There, there, there's nothing to be afraid of.' This may comfort us, but what does it really say to the child?

When we feel that the fear is inappropriate, it becomes harder still for us simply to let it be. Our own conditioning gets in the way. Were your fears always met with sympathy and respect? Or were you sometimes made to feel ashamed? Were you laughed at, or even punished?

The result of all this is that we collect a lot of confused, and confusing, messages about fear. We learn, essentially, not to trust our own responses. We learn to censor them and water them down. In particular, we learn that to scream and 'make a fuss' is more of a nuisance to our parents than to go quiet and withdraw. In other words, a passive fear response is more acceptable than an active one.

In the ordinary way, we sort out enough of these confusions as we grow, to emerge as fully socialised adults. Our original fear responses are acceptably muted, and we carry a lot of unspoken anxieties because we are too afraid to share them, but we get by. Most of us operate in this sort of way. In order to see more clearly how crippling the effects of unexpressed fear can be, we need to look at a more extreme example.

Elaine was thirty-five when she first came into therapy. Her marriage had broken down, and the present crisis was bringing some long-buried feelings to the surface. In addition, her three-year-old daughter was the same age as she had been when – she suspected, but did not yet properly remember – she had been abused by her father. All the pieces of the puzzle were there; it only remained for her to give herself permission to fit them together. For her, therapy was a safe haven where she could at last begin to see her life in its proper perspective.

According to her mother, Elaine had been a lively and precocious toddler. Somewhere between the ages of two and three, she had changed, becoming quiet and withdrawn. Elaine herself could not remember a time when she had not lived in 'a haze of fear', and her appearance reflected this; she was very thin, with long hair that shadowed her face, and thick glasses. Her voice was low and monotonous, and her clothes drab and concealing. As a child, she had been bullied by other children, who sensed her fear and were quick to take advantage of it. She was afraid of her parents, her teachers, her peers, and she suffered from constant nightmares in which she was always pursued by some terrible monster. Socially and physically inept, her one solace was reading, escaping into books or into her own intricate fantasy world.

Elaine had never questioned why she was so different from other children. To a child, things simply are as they are. It was not until she began her therapeutic journey that she began to see what a barren desert her childhood had been, and that there must have been some reason for all those terrors. Slowly, she began to explore, feeling her way through the obscuring haze, back to where it was thickest, where the strongest demons waited.

What she found there, when she finally took her courage in both hands and went voluntarily into that place, was the memory of being sexually abused, and almost frightened to death, by her father. The memory was the first thing to emerge; the feelings that went with it, the raw terror, the helpless outrage and the sexual shame, did not come through until some time later, by gradual stages. However, as she allowed herself to feel these feelings and own them at last, she went through an astonishing transformation.

The first change was an immediate and dramatic increase in her sexual energy, which had always been fairly low. Elaine had never been able to get properly angry before, had hardly even raised her voice; now, she learned how to shout and scream, and to stand up for herself. She discovered that the more people saw of her, the more they liked what they saw; and so she began to take risks, dressing more attractively (which had seemed an incredibly dangerous thing to do), expressing herself more openly. It had always been too dangerous for her to know her own feelings, let alone show them, and this had been a major cause of the failure of her marriage. Now, at last, she began to be capable of real relationship. In her own words, 'I feel as though I've lived most of my life in black and white, and now, suddenly, the world is full of colour.'

Fear is a paralysing force. In order to survive, Elaine had cut herself off as completely as she could while still living. The price she paid was enormous. Unexpressed and unacknowledged fear leaks out wherever it can, destroying our ability to act and react freely. When it comes to relationship, we are unable to flow, to be spontaneous; there is always a shadow, a hesitation.

It is normal and healthy sometimes to be afraid. But if you are often afraid, if it stops you from engaging with the world, or if you suffer from apparently meaningless terrors or panic attacks, remember: the terrors and panics do have a meaning. Fear does not arise without a cause. You do have a choice: you can honour your feelings, or try to suppress them. The quality of your life depends upon the choice you make.

ANGER: THE RED TIDE

Childhood rage is difficult for adults to cope with. It is noisy, chaotic, and potentially damaging to the child or to any people or things within reach. Moreover, the first rages usually arise when the child's wishes come into conflict with those of the parent, so the parent has to find some way of dealing with them without losing control. The child learns, fairly early on, that losing its temper rarely brings about any positive results, and that disapproval and dismay are probably the mildest reactions it can expect. And in later childhood the reactions get stronger; a child of ten who has a tantrum is likely either to be laughed at, or to be punished.

Our anger is therefore another emotion that we learn to be ashamed of. If we manage to suppress it, we grow up avoiding conflict as much as we can. When someone at work annoys you, do you find a way to tell them, or do you hold your tongue? If you do not tell them, do you tell other people in your workplace about it, or do you take it home to off-load onto your partner? If you do not talk about it at all, what happens to your irritation? Try as you will, you cannot simply make it disappear.

It will go underground, and it will affect you physically, tensing your muscles and inhibiting your breathing and hindering the free flow of energy. It will track sideways under the ground, and it will leak out wherever it can find a weak spot, usually when you are dealing with people of whom you are not afraid: your children, your partner, your nearest and dearest. It spills out clumsily, inappropriately, wounding those you love.

Is it not worth trying to learn a better way of coping with anger? For it is a potent force, a fierce expression of life energy. This is the energy that moves outward, that gets things done, that engages with the world. In many ways, anger and fear can be seen as opposite, or complementary, forces. There are those who say that, in order to live peacefully together, we must learn to renounce our anger. They have not understood that, if we could really do that, rather than simply suppressing it, we would also lose our ability to create, to do, to make and to mend. A person who cannot be angry is depressed.

Rather than trying to renounce it, we have to learn how to embrace it. As with fear, if we become familiar and friendly with our anger, we can come through to a place where it becomes an ally. Instead of being overwhelmed by our rage, we can ride it, and use it constructively rather than destructively. But there are no short cuts; we cannot just decide to do this. First, we must learn to express it, and honour our anger as it arises. Next, we must learn how to modify that expression, to become aware of the effect it has on other people. At the same time as we welcome home our own anger, so we become more comfortable with anger in others, more able to give them permission to express it, and less threatened when it is directed at us. Only then can we move on to the third stage, where we gain the power to use it as we wish.

Stage 1: Letting our anger loose

Quite often, we do not even know when we are angry. A common way to avoid feeling it is to side-step into something else, something more acceptable. For instance, I have a client whose husband is dying of cancer. In our first two sessions, the main emotion she expressed was a sort of wise sadness. She said she meditated a lot, and that she had good friends to whom she could talk about anything, and I was left feeling that, somehow, we had not really met.

In the third session, as we talked about how her husband was struggling with his feelings, I remarked that it must be very hard for her to be sympathetic all the time. Tears sprang to her eyes; she began to sob, and then burst out with, 'He's such a bastard to live with!' Immediately she tried to apologise, but this was a moment of truth, and in that moment she came alive. Her eyes brightened, her back straightened, and we made real contact for the first time. Her anger was not the whole truth, nor did it cancel out all her other feelings, but her shame and denial had given it more weight than it deserved, and so added to her burdens.

Another way to side-step our anger is to retreat into the head, and take the moral high ground of apparent reason and logic. It is infuriating trying to argue with someone who does this. While they remain cool, calm and puzzled by other people's inability to control themselves, everyone else is acting out their unexpressed rage for them.

I remember working in a group with Jonathan, a young man whose family, he said, never touched each other and never showed emotion. In the group, he would offer judgments to others based on how he thought they should behave, and he was bewildered by their hostile reactions. We looked at what had happened the last time he visited his parents, not having seen them for nearly a year. In passing, he mentioned that his father, after a brief greeting, had gone off fishing for the whole weekend. When someone asked if he was not hurt by this, he replied, 'Well, his fishing is very important to him.' There was a sort of collective hiss at this. Surely he minded, even just a little bit, that his father hadn't cared enough to spend ten minutes in his company?

Jonathan continued to deny that he felt anything about it, while all around him people were getting more and more agitated. In the end another young man, Adam, jumped up and asked if he could 'speak for' Jonathan to his father. Jonathan shrugged and said that was fine by him. Addressing a cushion as the father, Adam said 'Hi, Dad! Anybody in there? Hey, I'd like to talk to you. It really hurt when you went off like that. You hardly waited to say hello to me. Aren't I worth even five minutes of your attention?'

As he watched, Jonathan's face twisted in pain. He looked at his 'father' and said, 'Yes, it does hurt. You couldn't even be bothered to be there. Fishing was more important than your son. Pretty well everything is more important.' Suddenly he was sobbing, difficult, tearing sobs, and shaking with the force of the grief flowing through him. And with the grief came rage, all the helpless anger of a child not listened to, not interesting enough to be bothered with. It poured out of him incoherently, messily, and it was far easier to be with than his usual detachment had been, because it was real, and strong, and alive. Typically, Jonathan was afraid afterwards that he might have 'upset' people. Instead, he found that their anger had gone completely. Expecting to be 'told off', he found himself being congratulated.

In this first stage, when we are finding our way back into feelings that have been long suppressed, or barely held in check, we cannot be graceful in the way we express them. They just need to blast their way out. Our task is not to try to control them any more, but to find safe places where we can give ourselves permission to let go.

This often means a therapeutic setting, whether in a group or one-to-one, with a facilitator who understands how to prepare the way, and help to integrate the changes that will happen. However, it can also mean a strong relationship, where there is enough trust and commitment and wisdom to contain the blast. Once we go beyond the first stage of relationship, these feelings tend to arise of their own accord in any case, as the wounded spirit tries to heal itself. It is up to us whether we try to push them down, dump them onto our partner, or form the intention to work through them.

Stage 2: Riding the rapids

When we no longer have trouble giving free rein to our anger, then – and only then – can we begin to modify the way in which we express it. We must first learn to honour our own feelings, before we can truly be responsive to the feelings of others. In the second stage, we have to learn to take responsibility for ourselves, and to recognise that what we do with our feelings has a profound effect on those around us.

This is true of all feelings, but it is probably most obvious with anger. When you shout, people notice. You may be shouting at nobody, or at one person in particular, but everybody within earshot will be affected in some way. Some people – those most comfortable with their own anger – can handle it without being rocked too badly, but most will be upset in some way, and will react with fear, distress or anger in turn. It is almost impossible to remain indifferent.

And so we have to recognise, from a place of maturity and inner knowing that is very different from the sanctions imposed upon us as children, that we do not have the right to invade other people with our anger. Once the first urgency of self-expression is past, we must learn to choose the right times and places to voice our anger. We must also learn to modify it according to the recipient, if there is one. Some people are more easily wounded than others. Children are the obvious example, but all of us are more vulnerable at some times than at others. If you push too hard with your anger, you simply push people into putting up their defences, and then communication is lost.

Renata worked in a residential care community. Her work meant that she had to be in close and continuous contact with her colleagues. She had a history of abuse and other deeply wounding experiences as a child but, rather than trying to bury her anger, Renata was constantly living it. She would fly into a rage when she did not get her own way, and whatever other people gave her was never enough. After a time people simply avoided her whenever they could, and so she became very isolated. This was a familiar situation for her, and she was miserable in it, but she could not see any way out.

The whole community came to be dominated by Renata and her tantrums, until one person finally dared to risk challenging her, and to point out – in as loving a way as possible – that she was overwhelming everyone with her anger and driving them away. Somehow, the fact that he had cared enough to do this, at the risk of inciting her wrath, got through to her, and she was grateful.

Renata went into therapy, to begin the task of tracing her feelings to their source. Slowly, over a period of many years, she learned that she did not have to be angry to feel real. She began to be able to notice the onset of rage and, instead of immediately vomiting it over other people, she learned to take time, breathe deeply, and recognise whether it was an appropriate response to her present situation, or whether it arose from some older, deeper place within herself. At the same time, she became able to choose what to do with it: whether to express it immediately, and in what way, or whether to acknowledge it and move on. It can be a long, hard journey, but becoming mindful of others is the other side of honouring our own feelings. For relationship to be possible, the two must go hand in hand.

Stage 3: Catching the Bull

There is a Buddhist meditation that works directly with the energy of anger. Anger is a rising emotion. If you have time to notice, you can feel how it moves up through your body, from the depths of your belly to your head. It demands to be released through action of some sort. This happens whenever we get angry, and it is possible to contain this rising energy rather than discharging it. To practise the meditation, you need to sit quietly and clear your mind as much as possible. Begin by focussing on a person or situation that has made you angry, deliberately invoking the feeling, encouraging it to grow until it wells up inside you and fills your whole being. Let it build until just before the point of release – and then hold it there. Stay with it, breathing deeply. If you can contain the charge, a transformation happens. It no longer feels like anger that you are holding, but pure, intense life force.

This is called 'Catching the Bull', a name that reflects the way we usually relate to anger – as a dangerous, wild thing that must be penned in. This meditation enables us to harness that strength and wildness, so that it becomes a tremendous source of power and creativity. For anger is nothing more than vital energy, rising in response to blockage or frustration of some sort.

You don't have to practise the meditation to reach this stage, but you do have to be easy with the full and uncontrolled expression of your anger, and you do have to be able to modify it as well. As I said at the beginning of this section, there are no short cuts. It comes with long and hard experience. Two well known people come to mind, whom I believe to be masters of this art – though there are thousands of ordinary men and women who practise it, unobtrusively, every day. One is Nelson Mandela, and the other is the Dalai Lama. Both have every right to be enraged, not just over wrongs done to them personally, but over the horrors suffered by their people. However, they do not fulminate against their enemies, or incite violence and retribution. Instead, they use that energy, that passion, to inspire others and to create, rather than destroying. If they can choose to do this, then so can we.

GRIEF: THE CLEANSING RIVER

There is an image that sticks in my mind, as a potent illustration of the way our society handles grief. After a plane crash in which many people were killed, one newspaper carried a photograph of a child, a boy of about eight or nine, standing by the newly dug grave of his mother and father. The article that accompanied it praised him for his courage because, as he watched the burial of his parents, he had shed no tears.

What kind of courage is this? What kind of madness is it, that does not allow a child to howl and scream and rage at the loss of his parents? It is regarded as perfectly normal, in fact, not to take children to funerals at all – presumably in case it upsets them. It is also normal for people, especially women, to take tranquillisers when they are bereaved, to help deaden the pain. This is one time when our emotions can be so intense that we may feel as though we, too, will die if we do not express them, and yet still we do our utmost to keep them down.

Of course, a moderate display of grief is allowed, at least in the first few days following a major bereavement. It is quite acceptable for women, though less so for men, to cry at funerals. After a week or so, however, people no longer want to hear about it. They are embarrassed, and they try to talk about something more cheerful, or they avoid you altogether.

When it comes to the kind of loss that ranks lower in the scale, there is even less tolerance or understanding. Grief is a natural human response to any kind of loss, whether it be the loss of a loved one through death or departure, the loss of a job, leaving one home for another, the loss of health or hopes. Then there are the hidden losses that are hardly even acknowledged, the miscarriages and stillbirths and abortions, the ending of secret affairs. The loss of freedom and independence that comes to a woman when, however joyfully, she becomes a mother. The gradual, continual loss of youth and dreams and opportunities, as we choose one path rather than another.

What happens to this great weight of unexpressed grief? Does it work, to distract ourselves with other things or smother it with drugs? I am reminded of Alex, who was referred to me because for the last few months, for no apparent physical reason, he had lost all interest in sex. When we met, he told me that this started when his mistress of many years finally ended the affair, because he would not leave his wife. 'At first, I was depressed,' he said. 'But now I don't feel anything.' What he really meant was that at first he had been feeling his pain, but that now he had shut down his feelings, and his sex drive had gone with them. This is depression; and this is what happens when we deny ourselves the right to grieve.

I can illustrate the process best with another example. Serena came to therapy in her early fifties. She was an elegant, very composed woman, but in the last few years had become increasingly disabled by panic attacks and fits of crying. She could not tolerate being in crowds, and was unable to cope with conflicts, even minor ones. She said that she had been depressed for many years.

There were two obvious major traumas in her life. When she was in her early twenties and still living with her parents, her sister was killed in a car accident. The shock paralysed the entire family; a wall of unexpressed grief went up, and what had been a happy and vibrant family environment became sterile. Serena herself had been a carefree and fun-loving girl; now, she became much more serious and introverted.

A few years later, she met and married Daniel and, with her marriage, she rediscovered her joy in living. For ten years, they were very happy together. The marriage was brought to an abrupt end when Daniel discovered that he had a particularly virulent form of cancer, from which, after only three months of illness, he died. Serena 'coped', because she felt she had to, but what she did not do was to cope with her own agony. It was simply too much for her, and there were other people to look after, and things that had to be done – as there usually are. So she discounted her feelings, found ways of distracting herself. She took up social work, in an area where she was constantly dealing with grief and pain in her clients; but it did not help to discharge her own pain.

Slowly, over many months, we began to explore her grief. My job was to provide an environment in which she could do this, an environment that simply was not available to her in her everyday life. Witnessed and supported by me, Serena allowed herself to re-experience the deaths of her husband and her sister. She opened up the places that she had not gone into at the time, feeling what was there to be felt, and expressing what was crying out for expression. Week after week, she would spend whole sessions sobbing.

Sometimes it seemed that there was no end to her tears, that her fears were justified and that, once she had begun, she would never stop crying. Often, she would be torn between the need for release and the urge to close down, to feel no more pain. What kept her going was her own deeper wisdom; the sense that she was keeping faith with herself and with her own dead loved ones. And little by little, as Serena restored her grief to its rightful place, it stopped leaking into other parts of her life. The panic attacks, weeping for no apparent reason, mental confusion and fear of crowds all dropped away. So, gradually, did her sense of depression. She began to come alive again.

At the same time, healing was taking place. Over the months, her traumatic losses began to lose their paralysing power over her. She could remember the lives of her husband and her sister, as well as their deaths. Huge areas of her own life, that had become taboo because of their painful associations, now opened up to her again. Serena no longer sees it as a weakness to need therapy, for she is far stronger now than she ever was before. Three years on, she is training to be a counsellor herself, and she will be a wise and compassionate one. Unafraid of her own depths, she will be able to support her clients as they go into and through theirs.

You cannot possibly grieve too much. The body knows, and the spirit knows, when enough is enough. Our minds are not equipped to judge these things. Nor can you possibly make too much noise about it, whatever other people may think. In many other cultures, and particularly in less sophisticated ones than our own, it is part of the ritual of mourning to wail and to scream, to tear your clothes or even your own flesh in the intensity of grief. In the act of weeping – not just a few discreet tears, but the deep, loud, wrenching sobbing that can go on for hours – we shed more than we realise. There is a kind of ecstasy in grief, a loss of self that happens when we allow ourselves to go deeply into our pain, without holding back. In that place, there is healing.

The process of grieving after a major loss, if we allow it to happen without blocking, takes about two years to go through. For the first six months the grief is intense, and dominates our lives. Over the next eighteen months or so, healing and recovery will happen. However, if we do block the process, or distract ourselves – with work, new relationships, alcohol or drugs, and so on – recovery may never happen. We can carry our griefs for a lifetime, and a lifetime of grief is what we will have.

There is a beauty about someone who is truly grieving that is very different from the dull, heavy feeling of someone who is depressed. Once you are comfortable with your own capacity for mourning, it is not hard to keep company with those who have been bereaved. It can be deeply moving, even inspiring. What is difficult and uncomfortable is to be with someone who will not allow themselves to feel their own grief. It is there, unexpressed and unacknowledged, and it casts a pall over everything.

The implications for relationship are clear. To hold back grief is to dull the edge of feeling, and so to diminish the possibility of intimacy. To allow it, on the other hand, is to offer your partner a great gift. If he or she is able to accept it, both partners will be richer. If you can grieve together, then you can also rejoice together.

Coming Home To The Heartland

If I seem to have painted a very bleak picture, it is only to emphasise how far out of balance we are in the way we handle our emotions. Just as we deny and suppress them, so we deny the consequences of suppression. It is necessary to look fairly and squarely at the price we pay for that denial, in order to be able to learn a different way of being.

Once we do begin to look, the consequences are only too obvious, in terms of the immense problems that we have in simply relating to each other. The only way to redress the balance is to set about the task of learning to express ourselves freely and honestly. When we can do that, we can allow our partners to do it as well. In seeing ourselves more clearly, we can also begin to see other people, and to learn other people's languages in all their infinite variety. In other words, we can begin to communicate, and through communication comes intimacy.

6

Conflict Management: Riding the Storms

'As long as we are on earth, the love that unites us will bring us suffering by our very contact with one another, because this love is the resetting of a body of broken bones. Even saints cannot live with saints on this earth without some anguish, without some pain at the differences that come between them.'

THOMAS MERTON

Martin and Kim came to see me together. After nearly five years of marriage, they were about to split up. They were very polite to each other, very considerate, and I noticed that, when they talked about their troubles, it was always with a smile.

We began to explore the history of the relationship. It was sexual magnetism that had drawn them together, and the dreams that they shared: to travel the world, to have children. For about six months, they were in bliss. Then Kim became pregnant. She was delighted, but for Martin it brought up a lot of fear. He was afraid that their magical relationship would be weighed down by responsibilities, and he also thought he had to let go of the idea of travelling.

He could not share wholeheartedly in her joy. But, instead of talking about his fears, he withdrew emotionally, not wanting to upset her. Kim, of course, was both upset and angry at his withdrawal, which she did not understand; but she also tried to hold back her anger. Martin, sensing this in a thousand subtle ways, withdrew further. Into this troubled atmosphere their first child was born.

Their son was three years old by the time they came for counselling, and the gulf between them had grown so wide that they no longer felt there was a relationship to work on. Amicable separation was the most they hoped to achieve. Nevertheless, as we worked together, it became plain that there was a great deal of unexpressed hurt between them. When I invited them to speak some of their feelings to each other, Martin was very nervous and afraid. Kim, on the other hand, was excited at the opportunity to express her anger, and she felt that the therapeutic setting gave her permission, and a safe environment in which to do so.

As she opened up her store of long-held resentment, the automatic smiles disappeared. Martin's own resentment came to the surface, and he spoke about his fear and rage as he saw his dreams dwindling away. In the weeks that followed, they began to learn how to express their feelings, and to listen to one another. As they struggled to share their truths without tearing at each other, so an unexpected enjoyment of these spirited encounters began to grow. What had been a dry and arid relationship became a juicy one. Through the spark of conflict, the spark of love was rekindled.

Conventional wisdom says that relationships are destroyed by the wounds we inflict upon each other through what we say and do, but my observation is that the reverse is true: far more relationships break up over what is not said than over what is said. Today, Martin and Kim have a marriage that works. They are struggling with issues of freedom and commitment – and a host of other things – but they have both learned to bring honesty and passion into their everyday relating.

Conflict is an essential and healthy part of relationship. It is impossible to express ourselves and our needs without conflict. Intentionally or unintentionally, we hurt each other, just in the course of day-to-day living.

What can we do about it? In order to bring the art of conflict into its rightful place in relationship, we have to confront in ourselves the deep-rooted conviction that says: 'Conflict is wrong; quarrelling is a sign that something is amiss. If I were a better human being, or if you were less controlling, selfish, bad-tempered, we wouldn't need to fight. In a perfect relationship there is perfect harmony. Maybe I'm with the wrong person . . .'

All of this is rubbish, and not at all helpful when it comes to making strong, resilient, loving relationships. In trying to sweep conflict under the carpet or treating an argument as a major disaster, we lose a precious opportunity to learn a little more about each other, to become more intimate. And there is much more to the territory of conflict than we can possibly imagine from the sort of hit-and-run skirmishes around its edges that are the usual stuff of fights between partners. Here, too, there is tremendous potential for transformation, if we can only summon up the courage to stay with feelings and situations that are painful for us.

LEARNING THE LANGUAGE

Once again, it is a question of learning the language; listening, to yourself and to your partner, and noticing what you do when a clash happens. You can't stop to analyse what is going on when you are in the middle of it, but you can agree to do so afterwards, and to discuss it with others outside the partnership as well. The simple act of making an agreement like this – preferably not in the heat of the moment, but when both partners are cold sober – immediately begins to transform the way you approach conflict, and the way you handle it.

What is the language of conflict? At the simplest level, it arises when one partner tries to express feelings to the other, and is met with either hurt or anger, or both. Defences then come into play, and you will notice that you have favourite ways of reacting. All the many forms of defence can be put into two groups: those that involve withdrawal, and those that involve attack. Withdrawing means closing down, retiring hurt, refusing to talk any more, or – more subtly – trying to move the ground of the conflict, and arguing from your head or shaming your partner for getting into a state. Attacking means trying to wound, bringing up old scores, shouting, physically assaulting. There are, of course, infinite variations on these two themes.

Typically, an argument involves a confused and confusing mixture of tactics, with both combatants frequently shifting ground and trying to gain an advantage. It ends with the withdrawal or collapse of one partner, but both usually go away feeling wounded and morally superior. We may attempt reconciliation, but we tend to avoid inspecting the wounds too closely, lest we stir up further conflict. We try to smooth over the hurt, to forgive and let go and 'get back to normal'. The original injury is now overlaid with new ones got in the heat of the battle. No wonder conventional wisdom regards conflict as inherently bad and destructive for, unless we learn some better ways of handling it, it cannot be anything else.

This chapter deals with some of the ways in which we can begin to work constructively with conflict. It also looks at the art of forgiveness, or the healing of old wounds. I want to emphasise, however, that this is no easy undertaking. It is hard and painful work and, although we gain experience along the way, it will never be effortless. It is the effort itself, choosing to go through the agony again and yet again, that gives birth to love, and provides it with the nourishment it needs to grow.

DEALING WITH CONFLICT CONSTRUCTIVELY

As well as learning the language of conflict, and becoming comfortable with the expression of strong emotions, we need to set up a framework within which to contain it. Once we have certain structures in place, it becomes much safer to take risks, knowing that the relationship will not be blown apart. These structures involve: commitment, both to explore problem areas together and not to leave when the going gets tough; the intention to reach an outcome that satisfies both partners; an understanding of the importance of timing, in order to maximise the chance of a positive outcome; and a strong support system.

1. Making a commitment

The first step is to make an agreement that, when clashes happen, time will be set aside to look at what is going on. This means that both partners must be willing to explore their own dark places, and to work towards change. In other words, this is the point at which the issue of commitment arises.

Unless both partners are willing to grow with and through the areas where they run into trouble, the relationship will inevitably move towards compromise, stagnation or death. If they *are* willing, however, it is immensely helpful to make some conscious statement of commitment. This does not have to be 'till death us do part'; it simply means declaring our intention to stay with the process as it unfolds, not to cut and run when things get difficult.

This is a vital step towards establishing trust, and making it safe within the relationship for whatever needs to emerge. Just as becoming a parent means – in theory at least – making a pledge to be there for the new human being until he can be there for himself, so entering into mature relationship involves the same sort of commitment.

Having said this, I want to emphasise that, unless *both* partners are willing to commit themselves to growing and working with what comes up, there can be no deal. If you are living with someone who is abusive, physically or emotionally, and he or she is not willing to change, then you owe it to yourself to get out. There is no merit in allowing yourself to be abused, and no benefit for either partner if you stay. Unless each can give honour and respect to the other, the relationship cannot evolve.

Most of us find the idea of commitment a little frightening, and for many it is terrifying. We fear being trapped, shackled to someone who may turn out to be a nightmare to live with; and what if someone better comes along? I have seen so many relationships, on the brink of moving into a new and more mature phase, come to grief because one partner or the other could not bring themselves to commit.

However, it need not be like that. Some years ago, a friend of mine was considering training to be an osteopath. The course was four years long, full time, and Michael, my friend, had no prospect of financial help. The reaction of many people he knew was, 'How can you possibly make that kind of commitment? Who knows where you'll be in four years' time?' Michael said that, if he looked at it that way, the thought of those four years filled him with dread; but he had been drifting for some years now, not realising any of his dreams, and if he did not jump one way or another, he could still be doing that for the next four years. The only way to progress was to make the commitment, day by day and week by week, to be with what he was doing right now. He took the course, and finished it, and is now a successful practitioner. And along the way, his closest friends became those who were also willing to take the risk of throwing their energy into making their dreams come true.

It is the same when we make a commitment of the heart. All we can do is to pledge ourselves, as fully as we can, for this moment. However, in the making of a pledge like this, magic happens. When we really throw our energy into relationship – with the conscious knowledge that it will always be less than 100 per cent, simply because we are human – we create momentum. We create a place where the relationship can expand, and we can be open to the adventure and the wonder of it, as well as the burdens. If we give it as much as we can today, we are more than likely still to be here tomorrow, and next week; and it will not be the same. We will be moving, and growing.

What are we committing ourselves to? Simply this: to keep company with one another on our journey of self-realisation. As trust grows, and love grows, and we learn to express what we are feeling, so issues from our past will surface, seeking resolution. Unconsciously at first, we will play them out within the partnership. Conflict will arise, and in that conflict is the key to becoming conscious, owning what works for us and what needs to be discarded, and healing old wounds.

These things will begin to happen whether we commit ourselves or not. But, if we do not commit, there will be no container in which to hold them, and the relationship may well founder. Once the commitment is in place, we can begin to look at some other ways of containing conflict so that, rather than simply suffering it, we can begin to use it.

2. Forming clear intentions

With commitment, and the resolution to use our differences creatively, goes the need to form clear ideas about where we want our conflicts to take us. Again, this cannot be done at the height of the battle, but at some more peaceful time, preferably when neither partner is actively feeling hurt.

What it comes down to is forming the conscious intention to reach an outcome in which no one is the loser. Creative conflict is not about wounding, scoring points, getting revenge or emerging victorious. It is about reaching a 'win-win situation', a place where both partners feel heard and respected, even if they do not necessarily get what they were originally fighting for.

It means shifting the focus, from whatever the fight was apparently about – which is often just a hook for all kinds of other things, in any case – to the quality of the interaction that goes on before, during and after the engagement. It means getting better at listening, and at expressing our feelings so that we can be heard. At the root of conflict is hurt, on one side or on both and, if this can be honoured, through expression by one person and acknowledgment by the other, the charge will be defused. It is easy to tell when this has happened, because the energy goes out of the fight, and softer feelings come to the fore.

In relationship, the desire to attack or to wound another person always springs from our own pain. We may succeed in wounding them but, although that makes us feel strong, our pain remains unheard, and we have created an enemy. This is often at its most obvious in divorce proceedings, in which two people who once loved each other go all out to humiliate and blame and score all the points they can, while nursing their hurt and grief in private. Who – apart from the lawyers – really benefits from this? And who, in their heart of hearts, really wants it?

Forming the intention that both partners should emerge as winners brings about a radical shift in the dynamics of conflict. The intention will not automatically become the reality, but it is a step towards it. As the proverb says, 'To travel hopefully is better than to arrive.'

3. Choosing your moment

Timing can make an immense difference to the way we handle conflict. In Chapter Five I touched on the way in which, once we have learned to express anger freely, we have to learn how to modify that expression. When we are comfortable with feeling our own feelings, and capable of holding them until the time is right for their expression, we become far more skilled at conflict management.

Having said that, it is important not to leave it too long before saying what you need to say. If you allow things to build past the point where you are able to express them gracefully, then there is likely to be an ugly and explosive scene. We have all seen this happen in work situations, where people may hold irritations with each other for a long time, and then suddenly lose all control over something that seems trivial. To speak out, at the time and on the ground of your choosing, is empowering; to lose your cool, or allow yourself to be goaded into a reaction, is not.

You need to choose your moment. Remember that, in relationship, the most constructive outcome is that both partners 'win', so choose a time, as far as possible, when neither of you is in a hurry to be somewhere else, too tired or carrying other burdens, in a defensive state before you start, or when other people are around – children, for instance – with whom you do not feel free to say what may need to be said.

If you are the challenger, opening a dialogue which you know may bring up feelings of hurt or anger, then you must be generous; you are in the stronger position, and it will not help if you place your partner at a disadvantage. Recently, I went to dinner with some friends, and among the other guests were a barrister and his wife. During the meal, he made several disparaging remarks about his wife's lack of intellect and achievement, clearly looking for support among his friends there. Not only was he perfectly comfortable sparring in public, but he was also enjoying the fact that his wife was not. She was embarrassed, angry and hurt, but ashamed to show it in company, and so she got back at him in various covert ways, which made her appear shrewish and ungracious. Their sniping poisoned the atmosphere and did not improve anybody's digestion. This is something that couples who are in trouble often do, but trying to get support in underhanded ways like this does not achieve anything except more bad feeling.

We also need to understand that whatever we say or do in the heat of battle should not be given too much weight. Somewhere in the process of healing our self-esteem and attending to our own wounds from the past, we gain the ability to take things lightly. When we are attacked, we can see – sometimes – that the attacker is acting from a place of pain, and we no longer have to fall victim to it. And conversely, if we have hurt somebody – whether deliberately or not – we can find the grace and the generosity to apologise, or make amends.

In the middle of a red-hot argument, however, this is far beyond our reach – and it is perfectly all right that it should be this way. During a fight, people speak and act from their anger, their hurt, their guilt. We simply need to be mad for a while, to go 'out of our minds' and let it all spill out, clumsy and inarticulate and unreasonable and outrageous as it may be. Children do this beautifully, yelling insults and getting into a killing rage with their siblings or close friends – and parents too, if their parents are wise enough to let them – but they do not hold it against one another for long. Once the storm has passed, they will play peacefully together.

From this we can learn the wisdom of giving it time, of letting things settle after a battle, and not trying to hammer it out endlessly or take each other to task for what we said in anger yesterday. There is a kind of dance in conflict. After an engagement in which strong feelings have been aired, it makes sense to move apart for a time, to make some space and allow those feelings to subside. They are not the whole truth and, with time, other, gentler feelings will rise to the surface. It becomes possible to see the other person's point of view, even if you still do not agree with it.

Now is the time to come together again, to acknowledge the hurts that have been suffered, and to talk over the new thoughts and feelings that have emerged. Sometimes resolution happens without any effort at all, because self-expression was all that was needed. Sometimes there is a great deal of work to be done, if the conflict has uncovered issues that need to be worked on. The main point here is that the argument itself is not the end of the world, although it may feel like it at the time. It is part of a process, and that process takes time to unfold.

4. Getting support

The old way of dealing with disagreements was to avoid them as far as possible and, if it was not possible, to fight in private. In our culture, it is unusual to see people lose their tempers in public. When we do it, we feel that we have 'lost face', unless it is a case of righteous indignation. There is a general disapproval of people who 'air their dirty linen' in front of others, although doing it covertly, like the couple I described earlier, is actually very common.

Hence, we often find it very difficult to build a support network that can contain conflict. It is one thing to discuss your grievances with friends who will affirm you and pass judgment on your partner, but this does not actually help the relationship to grow. For that we need friends and counsellors who are willing to act as witnesses, who will reflect back to us their sense of what is going on. We need, at times, to use them as 'seconds', to be present while we try to disentangle the strands of hurt and pain in the relationship. Then, we can ask them to hold the boundaries of the engagement, interpret our words to each other, identify the patterns that emerge, and make sure that both sides have been expressed and heard.

In this area of relationship, more than anywhere else, we simply cannot do it on our own. It is one of the great tragedies of our time that, although relationship guidance is freely available through

Relate and other forms of counselling, people so often only turn to this resource in desperation, when it is already too late, and the relationship has been damaged beyond healing.

The time to call on the support of friends or counsellors is when you feel that things have begun to drift, and you cannot address the problem on your own. Perhaps you have tried to express your feelings and not been met, or perhaps you are afraid of what your partner's reaction will be. Get support; bring in a friend or friends, people who care about both of you, and whom you can both trust. Choose the time and the place, and give the issue the energy it deserves. Both the partnership and the friendship will be enriched in the process.

FORGIVENESS: GOOD HOUSEKEEPING

When we have been hurt by someone, whether it happened twenty minutes or twenty years ago, a bond is formed. Whether we acknowledge it or not, we invest energy in that person. If we do not or cannot choose to express our hurt feelings, then the bond remains, and it continues to take energy.

As human beings, we are constantly striving to be whole, to realise ourselves more fully. So it is that old wounds will ache from time to time, reminding us that they are not yet fully healed. And it is the peculiar property of intimate relationships, what makes them such an extraordinary vehicle for transformation, that whether we are aware of it or not, we will try to use them to settle these old scores.

If, for example, you had a teacher at school who humiliated you in some way, you would have had to swallow your feelings of shame and rage, or invite further trouble. These feelings leave a stain, a sensitive place; and when, years later, your partner says or does something that evokes that childhood wound, you will both be taken aback by the vigour and intensity of your reaction. In fact, you may well unconsciously set this up to happen.

If the whole process remains unconscious, your partner will feel unjustly attacked, and you will be left nursing your hurt. This business of 'dumping' on a partner happens a lot in relationship, and it is a repeated invitation to wake up, start to put your house in order and attend to old wounds. As we do start to wake up, as we honour our own feelings and learn our partner's language, it becomes more and more imperative that we undertake this work of forgiveness, for our own sake, and for the sake of our loved ones.

Forgiveness, then, is an act of cleansing; a sweeping out of dark corners, and a freeing up of energy that can be put to good use in the here and now. It does not mean turning the other cheek, practising saintliness and being 'nice' to your persecutors. In doing that, we do further violence to ourselves. Nor does it mean simply deciding to forget about it and get on with living. Before we can do that, there is a process that we must go through, and there are no short cuts. This process is outlined below.

FIVE STEPS TO FORGIVENESS

1. Being ready to forgive

You cannot forgive because someone else wants you to. The only valid starting point for forgiveness is the point where you have healed your self-esteem enough to know, however dimly, that not forgiving is holding you to your pain. Once, the feelings of anger and hurt, or the desire for retribution, may have helped you to survive, but now you have other and healthier uses for the energy invested there. So your intention is to free yourself, for your own benefit. If you still want reparation or revenge, you are not yet ready to forgive.

2. Honouring the pain

Before we can forgive, we have to honour our own feelings. If you have been wounded, you will feel hurt. Whether you are aware of it or not, you will also be angry. There may be a host of other feelings, too, depending on the circumstances. Our task is to allow these feelings to exist, without censorship and without trying to water them down. We may need witnesses, we may need help, and we will certainly need time. It can be done through therapy, and through a thousand creative projects: writing, painting, acting, making a garden.

We may need to go over the same ground again and again, slowly and patiently, reliving and releasing a little each time. Deep wounds cannot discharge all at once. There are layers upon layers of pain, old traumas overlaid by new ones. This work proceeds spiral-wise; there will be periods of remission, when the hurt fades and your attention is given to other things, and then it will present itself once more.

And finally, just as we need help to find our way in to our feelings, so we may need help in knowing when we have done enough to honour them. It is possible to get hooked on intensity, to find a kind of joy in fierce anger or deep grieving, that can be hard to abandon, especially if you have cherished these feelings in your heart for many years. They make you feel real, and alive; without them, what will you be?

I have been working for the last year or so with Martha, who is in her mid-twenties. When she was a young child she was sexually abused by her father, and she left home as soon as she could and broke off all contact with her family. Towards her father, she felt an intense rage and hatred. When she heard that he was dying, she rejoiced. He contacted her, wanting to make peace before he died, but Martha's reaction was one of contempt and furious rejection; let him suffer, as she had suffered.

One day, she brought with her a letter that her father had written. Until then, we had been following her feelings as they arose, and it seemed clear that she was far from ready to forgive. As I read the letter, however, a new picture of her father began to emerge. He wrote that he was truly sorry, that he was appalled at the damage he had caused, and that, if he could live his life again, things would be very different. There was no self-justification, nothing for Martha to hang her anger upon; simply a very moving appeal, not for her forgiveness, but for some kind of meeting before it was too late.

The letter seemed to me to be a statement of genuine repentance. Martha was furious, as usual, but it struck me that there was a hollow quality to her anger; she was clinging to it, wrapping it around her like a protective cloak. Protecting her against what? In asking the question, the answer became clear. Without her rage, who would she be? Behind the anger was terror.

It was a turning point in our work together, and the beginning of a new task: the building of a Martha who was much more than an abused and grievously wounded child. She did go to see her father, for she felt now that, if she did not, she would carry regret for the rest of her life. There was no Hollywood-style scene of last-minute reconciliation as he lay on his deathbed but, now that she was finding new ground to stand on where she was not his victim, they were able to meet, and there was healing in it for both of them.

3. Breaking new ground

Martha's story also illustrates another aspect of the forgiveness process. At the same time as we are giving our pain the attention that it deserves, we also need to expand our lives into other areas that are untouched by old wounds. This is not as paradoxical as it sounds. It does not mean finding distractions and trying to forget about it. Instead, it means making a conscious choice to widen our options, to strengthen the fragile, often almost stifled, self that says, this is not all of who I am. There is much more to me than being a victim.

In making this creation of space into a conscious spiritual practice, we reduce the impact of the wounding in our lives. We can allow ourselves to be nourished in whatever we choose to do, and we pave the way for the grace to come to us that will finally enable us to forgive.

4. Conscious forgiveness

Sometimes, as we proceed with the work of honouring our feelings and widening our horizons (steps two and three) forgiveness comes about, gently, of its own accord. This happened for Rose, who had been working for two years or so on the damage done to her by her father, who had physically and sexually abused her. To begin with, she had nothing but dark memories of her childhood. She painted a picture of constant bickering between her parents, rising unpredictably to violent rage, and she remembered no affectionate physical contact at all.

The intensity of her unlocked feelings had begun to diminish, and Rose was taking a break from therapy for a few months – focussing instead on 'real life', as she put it – when she began, unexpectedly, to recall memories that had a different flavour: moments of good parenting. They were accompanied by feelings of tenderness towards her father, with the understanding that he had been, in his way, no less a victim than she herself. She realised, with some surprise, that she had forgiven him.

However, we cannot count on this happening. If you have come to the point where you actively want to forgive, but you know that you cannot quite let go, a ritual of some kind can help you get through that last barrier. It is important to devise it yourself, or to take some part in creating it, so that you forgive exactly as much as you choose, and in your own way. It can be solitary, or you can use witnesses or other participants.

Ritual is a very potent tool for transformation. It provides containment, a focussing for our intentions and our actions, and it acknowledges the power of spirit, our own and whatever higher powers we choose to call upon, to take us through when we cannot manage on our own. It can be as simple as a prayer, or a symbolic act of letting go, such as burying or burning something that represents the past; or it can be as elaborate as your imagination allows.

I have been working with Vicky, who is sixteen years old. Three years ago, her mother killed herself, and since then Vicky had been in a frozen state, unable to grieve because of her suppressed rage, and unable to rage because of her terrible guilt. Together, we set up a ritual, in which she brought a picture of her mother, and lit a candle in front of it. The only instruction was that she was to talk to her mother, and to allow whatever feelings came up, without censorship. Because we had created a sacred space, removed from the everyday world, Vicky was at last able to let herself be with her feelings, in a way that had not been possible for her with her family, her friends, or myself as her counsellor. It was clear to her that she needed to forgive her mother for taking her own life and, with the help of the ritual, she was able to begin to do this.

5. *After forgiveness*

How do we know when we have truly forgiven? It is easy to pretend to ourselves, because we want to be generous and loving, but if there is still resentment, if old scores still come up when we are feeling vulnerable, then we have not forgiven. The mark of genuine forgiveness, as Rose discovered, is when other and softer feelings arise. Sometimes, we cannot even recall what we felt any more; the energy invested there has been freed, and put to other uses.

More often, however, we are left with a mixture of feelings. The hallmark of forgiveness is not so much that the hurt or anger is gone for good, as that it no longer holds us; we can feel it, acknowledge it, and move on. Then, we are as free as we can ever be from the tangles of the past, and available for intimate relationship in the here and now.

7

∞

Sexuality: The
Sacrament of Love

'Sexual energy is a physical expression of spiritual power.'
MARGO ANAND, *The Art of Sexual Ecstasy*

Human sexuality is a wonderful gift, one of our greatest sources
of joy and pleasure. It can engage us on all levels – physical, emotional, mental and spiritual – and it can be a powerful force for
transformation and healing. And, as with anger and grief and the
other manifestations of passion that we have looked at, we do not
find it easy, in our culture, to be straightforward and uninhibited
about expressing ourselves erotically. Once again, the teaching
we receive is inadequate at best; at worst it can be deeply damaging. Sexual energy, it seems, is simply too hot to handle.

The expression of sexuality is hedged about with shame and
guilt. As children, we are shamed for being angry, for being
afraid, for crying when we are in pain; but most of all, we are
shamed for being sexual. Yet the more we try to push down this
delightful, potent, body-centred force, the more we try to control
and contain and condemn it, the more it leaks and sometimes
floods into every part of our lives. We hold within ourselves a
simultaneous fear and fascination for our own bodies and our sexuality, and we carry this into relationship as well.

This is an enormous subject, and one that has much to teach us
about the way in which we close down our aliveness and limit our
potential for ecstasy; for sexual energy is a direct expression of

life force and, if we limit or suppress our sexuality, we also lose some of our vital energy. Here, we will focus mainly on sexuality within relationship. What are the patterns and expectations that we bring to relationship, and how do they keep us from discovering our full sexual potential? Why do long-term relationships so often lose their erotic charge, and how can we learn to rekindle it?

HANDLING OUR SEXUAL ENERGY

Within relationship, we have the opportunity – or rather, if we choose to work towards true meeting, the need – to heal our sexual wounds. Lovemaking can be a wonderful way of deepening the intimacy between partners, but it can also leave us feeling desperately alone. How can we learn to ask for what we really want? And if we do get what we want, how can we learn to receive it?

And finally, what lies beyond all this? Just as there are stages to go through in the management of anger, so there are many levels on which we can learn to handle our sexual energy. On the first level, we learn to express ourselves freely and spontaneously, healing our wounds and honouring our own physical needs. On the second level, we learn to modify that expression so that we can engage harmoniously with others; in other words, we open our hearts, as well as our bodies, when we make love. On the third level, we can learn to channel sexual energy, so that, as well as being a source of physical pleasure and a way of expressing love and intimacy, it can also nourish us spiritually, opening us to higher dimensions of our being.

Stage 1: Pleasing ourselves

When we plunge into puberty, most of us are totally unprepared for the tide of sexual energy that overwhelms us. What guidelines does society offer for dealing with this? For girls, a continuation of the denial of childhood sexuality: be as attractive and look as sexy as you can, but don't be sexual – and, preferably, don't have any sexual feelings. For boys, the picture is just as angst-ridden, but in a different way. They become the keepers of sexuality for their age group, since girls cannot or will not do so. But with precious little wisdom to draw upon from older men and women, they are dismally ill-equipped to handle it.

On the whole, it is easier for young men to please themselves, at least at the most superficial levels of sexual gratification. Women, on the other hand, are taught to please men. Rather than exploring their sexuality for their own pleasure, they are more likely to be persuaded or sometimes compelled into it by the men with whom they come into relationship. Thus, they learn to use their sexuality to attract men and get what the old social models say only men can provide: money, security, influence, children. And, of course, love.

It takes years of experience and struggle, in our male-dominated society, for a woman to truly own her own sexuality. Many never manage it at all, and that side of relationship remains, for them, forever in the shadows. Bringing it into the light is one of the greatest challenges, and one of the greatest opportunities for transformation, for women in our times.

Thus, the quality of our earliest sexual encounters is likely to be quite different for men and for women. Young men tend either to romanticise their relationships with girls and try to rein in their sexual energy, or they pursue sex at the expense of love. Quite often, they try both ways, but with different partners.

A good, if extreme, example is that of Daniel, who came into therapy at the age of thirty-four. He reckoned that he had fucked – his own word – almost 200 women, but he had no idea how to relate to them. What excited him was the chase, the seduction; his longest relationship had been with one woman who kept him 'courting' for about six months. Once he got them into bed, and the first intensity of passion wore off, his ardour would begin to cool, and boredom would set in. This would grow rapidly worse as his current girlfriend began to 'make emotional demands', as he put it, and he would move on within three months at most.

What brought him into therapy was the growing awareness (which he had tried to stave off for many years with drink and drugs and other distractions, including sex) that he was deeply unhappy. Some time back, one of his short-lived liaisons had resulted in a child and, although he now saw the baby and her mother very infrequently, this new and involuntary relationship had touched his heart.

Daniel was bewildered for, despite his cynical treatment of so many women, he still cherished the romantic idea that, somewhere, the right woman awaited him. With the right woman, there would always be high passion, and few emotional demands. Each time his current partner started to try to engage with him on a more meaningful level, he interpreted it as a sign that here was yet another needy soul who had managed to conceal her true nature for a short while, and not the right one after all. Where could he go from here?

The answer, of course, as Daniel himself was on the brink of discovering, was to allow his heart to open, and to move into true relationship. So far, he had used his sexuality to take him further from intimacy, rather than into it. He thought that in having sex with a woman, he was penetrating the core of her mystery, and engaging with her on the deepest possible level. Instead, each encounter left him feeling somehow cheated, still hungry, still unmet. He had begun to explore various avenues of personal growth, and he had come to the point where he could no longer blame his sexual partners for this lack of meeting. The old pattern no longer worked for him on any level, and so, despite his resistance, he was being forced to move on.

If Daniel's habit of focussing on sexual encounters and avoiding emotional involvement was not nourishing to him in the long term, then neither is the complementary pattern, that of using sex to try to get love. Women tend to do this more than men, and many a relationship begins – or is stillborn – when these two patterns come into collision.

Hayley, with whom I worked recently, is a woman who learned very early on to use her sexuality in this way. She had a waif-like, fragile beauty, the sort of 'rescue me' look that many men find irresistible. This was coupled with a feisty and unquenchable spirit, which had enabled her to obtain and hold down the job of a captain in the army, despite fierce competition. She had had many brief sexual relationships, both before and during her eight-year marriage, and she was very clear about their place in her life. Sex, she said, made her feel wanted. Never, since early childhood, had she been sure that her parents really wanted her; and, for a short time, attracting a new sexual partner would help her to forget her own secret knowledge that she was worthless. It also gave her power over men, although at the same time it distanced her from other women.

Hayley loved her husband, Rob, whom she had married not because there was a great sexual attraction between them, but because 'he was nice to me'. Other men used her sexually and then moved on; with Rob, there was no deep communication, but a sort of distant, undemanding kindness. She said that, during the eight years of their marriage, she had never seen him vulnerable.

Crisis came, in the form of breast cancer. After an operation to remove part of one breast, Hayley went away on holiday by herself, to recuperate and take stock. There, she 'fell in lust', as she said, with Philip, a very attractive man who was also able and willing to meet her emotionally – something she had never encountered before, and did not quite know how to handle.

She returned to her husband, for she was not yet ready to abandon the old security. Nevertheless, she could not simply forget Philip, for this was not like all her other affairs. Hoping to deepen her connection with Rob, Hayley told him that she thought she had fallen in love, but that she wanted to share her feelings with him as a way to open communication, and to put their marriage on a more honest footing.

He broke down and cried with her and, for the first time, they were able to be vulnerable together. But it could not last. The combined threat of opening up emotionally, and coping with sexual jealousy, was too much for him, and within two months he had left her, for someone Hayley described as 'a younger version of herself'. Hayley knew him well enough to know that his new relationship was no more real, in emotional terms, than their marriage had been, but his leaving was a clear statement that that was what he wanted.

Although she had left Philip and tried to win back her husband, Philip refused to leave her. In her despair with her illness and with the loss of her marriage, all her self-loathing came to the surface. She understood now that the way she had used her sexuality had simply reinforced her pain and isolation, and had alienated her further from herself. Philip saw her in her neediness and her vulnerability, and yet he still loved her. Slowly, painfully, Hayley was beginning to open her heart, and to find out what she really needed. For the first time in her life, she was ready to be met, both emotionally and sexually, by the same man.

Stage 2: Dancing with another

She was a stripper, working in a nightclub. He thought that, by marrying her, he would be assured of great sex whenever he wanted it. He was a New Age healer, helping people to deal with their emotional wounds. She thought that, by marrying him, she was gaining a true friend who would respect and understand her. When they split up five years later, she described him as 'the most selfish man I've ever met', and he complained that she had almost no interest in sex.

Again, this is an extreme illustration of the oft-repeated truism that 'women put up with sex for the sake of marriage, and men put up with marriage for the sake of sex'. Like all truisms, this is a gross over-simplification, but it points the way into the next phase of relationship. When two people first become a couple, the sexual energy between them is often one of the major factors that brings them together. The flames rise high, for women just as much as for men. However, as the partnership moves into a more committed phase, habits are established, history begins to accumulate, and the sexual energy begins to die down, or even to disappear altogether. What is really going on here?

The superficial answer, the one that Daniel opted for, is that the magic has gone, and the relationship is over. On a slightly deeper level, we may not want to give up on it altogether, but we allow limits to be set. Compromise is born. Of course, this line of reasoning runs, you can't expect high passion for ever more. Now that we are staying in together instead of going out together; now that we are doing grown-up things, like sharing a home, pooling our financial resources, having babies, it's only to be expected that there will be less excitement, not just sexually but in other areas too.

All this is true, but it also misses the essence of what is happening. As a partnership grows, its focus changes. We may start with the heady delight of being in love, or the white heat of sexual magnetism, or the marriage carefully arranged to give us the best prospects in the long term; but we do not stay there.

There is in all of us, even the most cynical and selfish and frightened, a desire to open our hearts to another. At the centre of true relationship is a heart-to-heart meeting. We may think we have found this meeting when we fall in love, or in lust, but the heart is not fooled for long. And when this movement towards emotional communion is blocked or hindered – as it nearly always is, for one reason or another – it hurts.

What we do with that hurt, and how we may go about healing it, has been explored in other chapters. Here, the point I want to make is that sexual energy does not flow easily when there is an atmosphere of hurt, expressed or unexpressed. As the relationship grows, our old wounds begin to demand attention, and new wounds are inflicted as we struggle to balance our needs and desires.

Sexuality does not exist in isolation; rather, it comes to serve as a kind of barometer of the emotional health of the relationship. If we do not begin to attend to our emotional needs, the sexual meeting between us will also suffer. It is normal, and natural, for this to happen, and it is part of the process of moving closer together, rather than a sign that things are falling apart – although, if we are not willing to go with the process of heart opening, we may choose to take it that way.

There are two aspects to the art of learning to dance together in a sexual way, and both are concerned with communication. The first, which is the subject of countless sex manuals, is the art of pleasing each other physically. In bed, more than in any other area of relationship, we often expect our partners to be telepathic, or at least superbly tuned in to our needs and responses. Sometimes it happens that way but, more often, we need to work at it.

Other people's bodies are a mystery, whether your partner is of the opposite sex or not, and it takes time to learn the ways of pleasure. It takes time to develop trust and openness, especially if, in the first delight of meeting, you have let things pass that really do not work for you. We have to allow ourselves to be taught, as well as to perform; and if we have something to teach, we have to learn to do it gently, playfully, with generosity – not 'You're doing it wrong!' but 'That doesn't really work for me. How about trying this?'

The second aspect is the meeting of hearts. If your sex life has become routine and boring, or dwindled away to the point where making love has become an exceptional event, rather than being part of the normal flow of life, then, besides exploring ways to make it more exciting, you also need to put your emotional house in order. In a stable relationship, lovemaking grows from closeness.

I have a vivid memory of working in a group with Mark, who came full of anger and frustration because his wife, Lisa, hardly ever wanted to make love. I asked him to describe a typical day in their household, and he spoke of working at full stretch, coming home exhausted, dealing with children and supper, and having very little space for himself. Meanwhile, Lisa was also working part-time, looking after their two young children – one of whom was still breastfeeding – and running the house. At the end of the day, usually when she was in the bathroom getting ready for bed, he would approach her, try to give her a hug, and ask to make love. Lisa, knowing what was coming, would stiffen as he touched her, and then say that she was very tired and didn't feel like it. He would retreat, angry and rejected, and she would withdraw into herself.

As this scenario unfolded, there were murmurs of recognition from other group members, both men and women – including myself. Here were two people, both pushed to their limits, neither getting enough support from each other or from anywhere else. Between them ran a river of resentment, hurt feelings and unmet needs, and it was getting wider. Is it any wonder that Lisa, less able or willing to split her emotional and sexual selves, should not want to make love with Mark?

We have all been here, if we have been in relationship for any length of time. It happens when communication starts to dry up, when we begin to feel hard done by, or to take each other for granted. It is usually, though not always, women who lead the way, because women tend to find it harder to flow sexually when their hearts are not in it. And it is yet another invitation to wake up, to begin the work of relationship.

When we approach each other sexually, we have to learn how to come from a place of fullness, rather than neediness. Looking to another to meet our needs may be all right for a while, as long as we do not want to go deep. But in the long term, *it does not work*. It is only when we have healed ourselves enough, and developed our own inner resources enough, that we can truly come together. Then, relationship happens delightfully, creatively, arising from the overflow of energy between us. Rather than grasping at each other to try to fill our emptiness, we can truly dance together.

A note on celibacy

In one of the tabloid papers recently, I saw an article about a couple who were both well-known actors. The headline screamed, 'No sex for a year!', as though this were one of the biggest disasters that can befall a partnership. In fact, periods when our sexual energy seems to disappear or go underground are very common, whether we are in relationship or not.

It happens for a variety of reasons. Obviously, some kinds of physical illness affect our libido, and so does clinical depression. A major trauma, such as a bereavement or an operation, can cause it to disappear; and being a victim of sexual abuse, whether as a child or as an adult, is a common cause. In fact, being a victim of violence in any form, from seeing active service in the armed forces to having a car accident – anything which is, or seems to be, beyond our control – can lead to loss of libido.

In all these examples, while there is work to be done to heal the trauma, we also have to accept that the body has its own wisdom, and that it may be necessary to be abstinent for a time. There may be no obvious cause, and yet it happens, and it is something that we must make space for in a committed relationship.

The most likely time for celibacy to become an issue between partners is when they start a family. It is very common, and completely normal, for a woman to lose interest in sex, sometimes for two or three years, after she has had a baby. In many tribal societies this is recognised and respected, yet here it is one of the factors that often leads to the breakdown of the marriage. In becoming a mother, a woman is forced to grow up rapidly, learning to stretch her resources beyond her previous limits; and, for a while, her vital, and hence sexual, energy may become focussed upon her child rather than upon her partner. There may well be survival value for the child in this, in that it delays the arrival of younger siblings.

Meanwhile, enormous demands are also made upon the father, in that he is required to support both his partner and his child, not just financially but also emotionally. Giving emotional support is a skill that many men do not get around to learning before they become fathers (along with putting someone else's needs before their own, and practising sexual abstinence). It is no wonder that we often balk at this fence, and start looking for a new partner who – at first – will be more accommodating.

So much shaming goes on in our culture, both of women who do not want sex, and of men who try to compel them, or go looking elsewhere. In blaming each other for being as we are, we dishonour ourselves. There is no easy answer, except – somehow – to go through it. And if we do stay with it, keeping our hearts open, feeling and communicating and respecting each other, we will come through. There are vast rewards for doing so, in terms of making the relationship deeper and stronger, both sexually and emotionally.

Stage 3: Sacred sexuality

Like anger, sexual energy is a rising force; and, like anger, it can be channelled. But, whereas we have to learn to express our anger freely before we can learn to channel it, we can work with sexual energy in different ways at the same time.

The first way that most of us learn, whether through self-pleasuring or making love with a partner, involves the building of a sexual charge in various ways, and then its discharge through orgasm. Afterwards, the excitement dies down; energy has been spent. It is quite possible never to go beyond this level of sexual experience. However, if you have ever made love for hours at a time, or with a partner who is very special to you, or if you have explored the Tantric arts, you will know that there is much more to sexuality than that.

Through sexual activity, we can experience the feeling of being deeply connected, not just with a partner but with the whole of existence. We can experience heightened states of physical, emotional and spiritual bliss that go far beyond orgasm; and travelling to these places leaves us replenished, rather than depleted. Such experiences are akin to those of the great spiritual mystics, and they are accessible to all of us.

The key to these possibilities lies in learning to hold the sexual charge, rather than defusing it through orgasm, and moving it up through the energy centres of the body, using it to open our hearts and our spirits and our connection with the universe. It may happen spontaneously, but we can also teach ourselves how to do it at will. There are various bodies of teachings (see under Further Reading), notably those of the Tantric traditions in India and Tibet, of Taoism in China, and of the Native Americans, that have developed techniques for working with sexual energy in this way.

There are some common threads that emerge in all these teachings that have a direct bearing on the way we handle sexuality within partnership. The first is the invitation to recognise the divine spark in ourselves and in each other, and to know that, when we make love consciously, we can become gods and goddesses. This introduces an element of play into our sexual activity that can be both healing and refreshing; and it inspires a deep sense of honour, towards ourselves and towards each other, that can transform our sexual encounters, enabling us to be in our power and to transcend what we thought were our limits. It also spills over into other aspects of relationship for, once you have seen the god or the goddess in your partner, it becomes harder to abuse them or to take them for granted.

The second is the acknowledgment that, in the realm of sexuality, *women lead the way*. Tantra teaches that the goddess Shakti is the initiatress; she sets the pace, and Shiva must follow. Women are the source of life energy, and they hold an inexhaustible supply; in order to share in it, men must learn to please them reverently. The Native American teachings say that women have a head start on men, being less genitally focussed and more heart-centred, and that it is easier for them to attain the higher levels of sexuality.

Once again, we in the West have it backwards. With our patriarchal legacy, through which women have been completely sexually disempowered, we have shut down a huge part of our sexual potential. It is time for men to give away power, and for women to take it up. When we can do this, we will all be immeasurably enriched, not just in our sexuality but in all aspects of our lives together.

The third and last point is an assertion which appears in the teachings of the Native Americans. They believe that whereas making love at the lower levels depletes our energy, when we attain the higher levels, we nourish, not only ourselves, but the earth as well. In other words, we make this journey not just for our own benefit. In doing it, we give something back to the planet; a small return for all the resources that we use in our everyday living.

Those who have been there have experienced the reality of this. But, whether you believe it to be literally true or not, it makes sense to think that, in our striving to become conscious and to learn to relate from the full spectrum of our human potential, we might also be learning to heal our separation from the earth and all the other living beings that share it with us. To put it very simply, we are beginning to come of age.

8

Towards Mature Relationship

'I slept and dreamt that life was joy,
I awoke and saw that life was service,
I acted and behold, service was joy.'

RABINDRANATH TAGORE

There is no blueprint for what we are trying to create. Our only touchstone is our own humanity. As the old structures of family and religion fall away, we are being forced to find wisdom within ourselves. If we are to make relationships that are strong and lasting, that can hold us in our joy and in our pain, in our ecstasy and in our despair, and in all the less exciting places in between, we must learn to weave them from the substance of our own hearts and souls. There is no room for what we think we ought to be, but only for what we are.

What we are, and what we have the potential to be, is far more wonderful than any of the fantasies we can conjure up. When we make a relationship we need to start out with a picture of the Other that is drawn partly from reality and partly from our own fantasies. Equally, it is necessary to let go of the fantasies, to be disillusioned. As we do this, as we learn to accept the reality of the Other, so we free ourselves, and them, to unfold more of our potential.

It is as though we begin the relationship in the Garden of Eden, believing that we can dwell forever in paradise with our beloved. To attain maturity, we have to be cast out of the garden and be stripped of our illusions. In the process, we begin the work of creating Heaven on Earth.

Some years ago, I was asked by Richard, who had come to one of my groups, to work with him and his wife. When they first married they adored each other. Now, ten years on, he was in despair, feeling that there was nothing left of his marriage except the outward appearance. His wife, Sarah, never wanted to make love, was tired all the time and seemed only to want him as a provider and to take the children off her hands when he was not working. He had just started an affair, and said that, after all these years of marriage and drudgery, he had found someone who could meet and enjoy his passion.

When he and Sarah first came to see me, they seemed to fit the picture he had painted. He was full of nervous energy and feeling, while she was drab, slow-moving, and said very little. I had the sense, however, that a great deal was hidden below the surface. Almost at the end of the session, having worked quite hard to bring her out, I remarked to Sarah that she had the potential to be a beautiful and dynamic woman. Richard laughed scornfully, while she looked at me as though she could not believe what she had heard.

Over the next few months, I worked with them both together and separately, and I began to see a very different picture. Richard was angry with Sarah for not being what he wanted her to be, and yet, when she did shine, he missed it. She loved to sing, but her singing irritated him, so she had fallen silent. She enjoyed dancing, but he did not, and always wanted to leave early when they went to a party. Little by little, she had faded, until he had almost lost her.

Through therapy, Sarah began to regain her self-esteem, and to enjoy herself again. Grudgingly at first, Richard learned to accept, and to respect, the woman to whom he was married; and as he did so, their relationship, which had contracted almost to nothing, was able to expand. There was love between them, underneath it all; and, as they worked through some of the tangles they had got into, it began to grow. He came to understand that, if he wanted her to meet his passion, he also had to learn to meet hers; and, as I had glimpsed in that very first session, she had passion in plenty.

This is not a fairy story, and they certainly did not live happily ever after. Instead, they grew up. Growing up means seeing clearly, and accepting what we see. We may not like everything about each other but, if we can learn to let it be, then we make space for magic of a different kind. We can allow ourselves to be more than we thought we were; we can play with possibilities. And from acceptance comes respect, and affirmation. Not only can we allow each other to be what we are, but we can also help each other to expand. Being grown up means being able to be childish, to be silly and playful and passionate and sensible, and also to be divine.

WHAT IS MATURITY?

I cannot give a recipe for mature relationship, because I do not believe that there is ever a point at which we actually get there. At this stage in my life, I feel that I have arrived at a place beyond illusion and disillusion, where my relationship with my partner is nourishing to both of us. Where we go from here, I don't know. I strongly suspect that, if we are still together when we are in our eighties, we will still sometimes hurt each other, and misunderstand each other, and get it wrong. My hope is that we will continue to get better at moving through these places, and that we will spend more time enjoying ourselves together.

However, even if there is no recipe to follow, there are ingredients which seem to be common to long-term relationships in which both partners are committed to becoming more alive and awake, rather than finding a comfortable pattern to settle into. One of them, as we have seen, is the readiness to let go of what we thought we wanted and embrace what is really there.

Another is the acceptance of conflict, and the willingness to work with it. This requires us to use, and to refine, all the skills at our command; it means being able to espouse our own position passionately and wholeheartedly, taking the risk of getting it wrong and losing face, and also being able to let go of that position, to move with the flow of the argument, towards resolution and new knowledge.

Again, *both* partners must be willing. At any stage in a relationship, if one partner wants to explore new possibilities and the other does not, then the first partner is left with a choice: to accept the status quo, to leave, or to try to create an environment in which the other may choose to come with them on the journey. We cannot change others, but we can, with love, invite them to change themselves.

Another ingredient is commitment, the vessel in which the relationship is held, that enables us to dive deep and to fly high. I could make this list longer, but I have chosen to highlight those aspects of relationship which we are often unwilling to accept. There are many others, of course, which come more easily. At the root of them all is the willingness to meet, heart to heart, body to body, soul to soul; and, for an intimate partnership, the heart-to-heart meeting is both the beginning and the end of the journey. From it, from the flow of love between two people, everything else arises. The opposite of love is not hatred, but indifference.

How can we find the courage, the fierce passion of the heart, to keep cutting through all the tangles of hurt and misunderstanding and inertia that come between us? The answer, as always, is to turn back to ourselves, and to clear away the undergrowth that comes between us and our own heart's delight.

We all started out, as children, wide open and undefended. We were all born with the ability to reach for what we wanted and fight for it, to rage and rejoice and be quietly happy. We all learned, as we grew, to defend ourselves from hurt, to resent and to manipulate and to feel unloved. And we all need to find our way back to the full spectrum of our feelings; we need to choose, and keep on choosing, to open up rather than shut down, to follow the path of life rather than the path of death. Every time we make this choice, we allow ourselves a little more aliveness, a little more capacity for love; and, in so doing, we make ourselves a little more available for relationship.

PHASES IN RELATIONSHIP

It seems to me that there are three phases in intimate relationship: illusion, co-dependence and maturity.

1. *Illusion*

In the illusion phase, we reach out to another who seems to embody those extraordinary or magical qualities for which we yearn. This is where romantic love belongs, and where many – though by no means all – partnerships begin.

2. *Co-dependence*

The second phase is that of compromise; still seeking our own completion through partnership, we try to avoid areas where we clash, and look to each other to make up for our own shortcomings. Contracts are drawn up, consciously or otherwise: you make me feel safe, not lonely, and I will provide for you. You do the feeling for both of us, and I will do the thinking. I love your sparkle; you love my solidity. We complement each other.

This phase, which is sometimes called co-dependence, is an inevitable part of partnership. It enables us to do what we cannot do on our own. On the practical level, for instance, it provides the conventional framework within which to start a family: the woman gives birth to and cares for the babies, while the man provides for them. However, unless we can also move beyond it, it stifles our growth and holds us to patterns which keep us incomplete, unfulfilled. What starts out as a fair exchange becomes set in stone; we 'give' certain qualities or roles to the other person in the partnership, only to find that we cannot then have them for ourselves. If one partner seeks to change, the other is threatened, and the equilibrium is lost.

The system lacks flexibility, and this tends to show up at times of crisis and change, when new strategies are needed. In the ordinary course of events, every partnership encounters some of these crises: the birth of children, illness, job changes or loss of work, attraction to others outside the partnership, looking after elderly relatives, and death. These difficult times are invitations to take another step into maturity, to look within and to cultivate our own potential, our own resources.

3. Maturity

And so, out of these hard times, when our coping mechanisms break down and the old structures fall apart, comes the third phase of relationship. As we allow ourselves to feel our own pain and our own despair and, as we begin to take responsibility for our own healing, so we begin to release our partners and our friends from the old contracts.

It is not that we stop needing other people; on the contrary, the need for loving and truthful friends and companions is a theme that has come up again and again. What happens is that we stop needing them to complement us, to complete us. When we meet another person, we come to that meeting from a place of fullness, rather than emptiness. And, if we do not need them to supply something that we lack, or to play some part in our movie, then we can allow them simply to be who they are. This, in itself, is profoundly transformative.

CRISES IN RELATIONSHIP

It is worth looking at some of the crisis points in more detail, for each, in its own way, represents an invitation to try out a new way of being. The three that seem to hold the most potential for change are: having children, having affairs, and the ending of the partnership through death. How can we respond to these invitations?

Having children

The first point about having children is that it is a summons to grow up, to make ourselves and all our resources available to a new and totally dependent being who, for a time at least, will dominate what was once a partnership. No one is ever ready for this, and not many of us can answer the summons wholeheartedly, however joyfully we welcome parenthood. As with other aspects of relationship, we learn on the job.

And it goes on, long past the first skills needed to care for a new baby. As the child grows, it requires us to cultivate patience, to slow down, to draw upon our creativity and our diplomacy, to withdraw our projections and fantasies and let it be its own self. A friend of mine, who had spent a lot of time and energy travelling around to hear the teachings of various spiritual masters, said that it struck him with the force of revelation when he came home to his wife and two-year-old son that his teaching had been right there, waiting for him, all the time. If we can only find the courage and the humility to let them take the lead, our children can teach us so much of what we need to know.

The second point is that, even as having children invites us to take a step into adulthood, it also invites us to rediscover our own inner child. Through their freshness and spontaneity, their wonder and delight, we can find our way back to our own. Through their ability to flow with their feelings, they remind us what we have lost, and show us what it means to be whole. For this teaching, too, we owe them our gratitude.

Having affairs

We have seen that a strong and healthy partnership exists at the centre of a many-stranded web of relationships. We need friends to challenge, support and nourish us. Intimacy is not exclusive; the more friends we have with whom we can open our hearts, the easier it becomes, and the less satisfied we are with friendships that are not open-hearted. And yet, if we can be emotionally and spiritually intimate with others when we are in partnership, what is different about physical intimacy?

There are no easy answers here. What works for one couple may be a disaster for another. For me, the touchstone has to be the love and respect at the core of the partnership. If being sexual with someone else means keeping secrets from your partner, then deception has come upon the scene, open-heartedness is no longer possible, and energy is being taken out of the partnership. If, on the other hand, we can be as open about our sexual attractions or encounters as we can about any other kind of connection with others; and if we can stay open, dealing with whatever hurt or jealousy or confusion arises, then this too can be a rich opportunity for the relationship to go deeper.

My own feeling is that, more often than not, we are drawn to make sexual connections outside an established partnership when we perceive a lack of something – sexuality, romance, adventure – within it. In other words, the affair arises from a place of hunger, or emptiness. It may feed the hunger, but it also enables us to avoid looking at what is going on within the partnership. If we take our passion elsewhere, the vital energy at the heart of the partnership is bound to suffer. Once again, therefore, the temptation to be 'unfaithful' offers us the opportunity to wake up, and to put our own house in order.

Facing death

It may sound nonsensical to speak of death as an opportunity to deepen a relationship. Certainly, when one partner dies suddenly and unexpectedly, there is nothing to do but mourn. However, it is not so unusual to have some warning that death is approaching. A similar situation arises when a couple is facing a prolonged parting, for whatever reason.

The temptation is to try to tie up the loose ends, to 'make the most' of the time that is left. What this means is that, once again, all that is difficult or might lead to conflict must be suppressed. For the sake of a beautiful ending, we choose to withhold our truth. And what is so desperately sad is that, in making this choice, we begin to die to each other long before the moment of death arrives. I have worked with many people who are dying, or who are close to someone who is dying, and the loneliness they have to bear, in censoring what they say and what they feel, can be heartbreaking to witness.

What would happen if, instead, we used this awareness of death or departure to sweep away the barriers between us? If, with nothing more to lose, we chose to be fully alive to one another? I worked with one couple who made this choice, and their relationship went through an astonishing transformation in a very short space of time. John and Julie were in their forties, and had been together for seven years. She was one of the most passionately alive people I have ever met, and when she suddenly discovered that she had a malignant brain tumour and would probably be dead within a year, her chief response was rage. She turned her anger upon John, and upon anybody else who tried to get close to her. The only options for him were to withdraw, or to weather the storm.

Up until this time, John and Julie had enjoyed some of the best things that partnership has to offer. They were financially comfortable, well matched physically and mentally, and still in love with each other. Theirs was a passionate, volatile relationship, and neither was afraid of conflict. In the past, however, Julie had tended to resolve it – or rather, not resolve it – by leaving. Dramatic exits were her speciality.

Now, she could no longer do this. Instead, it was John who tried to take the edge off the intensity of the situation, using cigarettes and heavy drinking to dull his feelings. But she would not let him get away with it. Fired by the knowledge that time was running out, she would have none of the kindness, the tactful avoidance of pain, that is the usual lot of the terminally ill. She fought for her life, and she fought for the life of her relationship, in a way that was both painful and awe-inspiring.

John stayed the course. Initially, he had done his best to support her in her search for healing, concealing the knowledge given to him by the doctors that it was hopeless. However, he came to feel that, by withholding the truth, he was doing Julie no favours. What mattered was the quality of the time they had left, rather than its quantity. Bracing himself to meet her fury, he gave her the full prognosis.

Julie's response was extraordinary. At some instinctive level, she knew that death was imminent. Once that knowledge was

shared, she was able to stop fighting. Instead, she directed her for-
midable resources into the process of dying, embracing it with the
same passion that she had brought to her life. Within a week or
two, she was spending much of her time in a state of profound
meditation. Visiting her felt like being in the presence of the Dalai
Lama and, when I left, I took with me a sense of serenity and wonder that would last for some days. John describes walking along
the beach with her, very slowly, simply being and observing, lost
in reverence.

In those last few weeks, Julie healed her life. Together, she and
John were able to transcend many of their old stumbling blocks,
and their relationship came to maturity. They achieved a profound
respect for each other that was a rare privilege to witness; and this
came about simply because, rather than living in denial of death,
as we all do most of the time, they chose to embrace it, and to be
open to all the new possibilities that this brought them. Along with
the inevitable pain and sorrow, they found an amazing joy and
grace, an intense aliveness that carried them far beyond their ordinary limits. Perhaps, if we were able to honour death as our constant travelling companion, we could all find the courage to be
fully alive.

HEAVEN ON EARTH: AN
IMPOSSIBLE VISION?

Is there any meaning in all this, beyond our own search for happiness? Do we undertake this work simply for our own sakes? I
think not. I think that much of the struggle involved in learning to
live with another is about fully embracing their reality, without
losing our own. As we get better at this, it becomes less and less
possible to try to control them, to abuse them, to make them play
parts in our movie. We become free to meet, and to love, and to
honour.

If we have children, the work takes on a new urgency, for we
are their role models, and they will be the men and women who
inherit the Earth. We do it for them, too. We do it for all our com-

panions on the road, for when one person takes a risk, or tries out a new way, it becomes a little easier for everyone else. And we do it for the Earth, our Mother; for, when we truly open ourselves to the reality of others, just as it becomes impossible to use and abuse the people around us, so it also becomes impossible to exploit, to cause needless destruction and pain, to the Earth and to the other living beings with which we share our planet. We become 'responsible' in the true sense of the word; able to respond, and to repay some of the energy that has been so freely invested in us.

This is what I mean by creating Heaven on Earth – not a mystical, but a highly practical vision, for we on this small planet have to learn to live together somehow, for our lives' sake. And here, in our own homes, with our own partners, is where the learning begins. From the quest for true intimacy, our spirits gain the power to soar free. Through the day-to-day practice of truthful relationship, we can create a spiritual path that answers the needs of our times.

This is what is behind our yearning for relationship, behind the desire for security, the need for love, and all the other expectations we load onto the fragile bonds we make with other people. We may come through to a place of genuine intimacy for only a few moments at a time, but there is a fierce delight in true meeting. It cannot be confused with anything else, and it feeds us at a very deep level. Once we have tasted this delight, we become unwilling to settle for anything less.

In practice, in everyday relationship, we are constantly moving in and out of different ways of being. But I believe that, if we are committed to growing and becoming true to ourselves, we start to find that place more often. Eventually, we learn to come and go at will. And when we are there, all the needs and doubts and insecurities fall away. Then, we know that we have come home.

Further Reading

Relationships

John & Kris Amodeo: *Being Intimate: A Guide to Successful Relationships* (Arcana 1986)
Robert Johnson: *The Psychology of Romantic Love* (Arcana 1983)
Barry & Joyce Vissell: *The Shared Heart* (Ramira 1984)

Personal development

Bandler & Grinder: *Frogs into Princes* (Eden Grove Editions 1979)
William Bloom: *Meditation in a Changing World* (Gothic Image 1987)
Freedom in Exile: The Autobiography of the Dalai Lama (Hodder & Stoughton 1990)
Ram Dass & Paul Gorman: *How Can I Help?* (Rider 1985)
Erich Fromm: *The Art of Loving* (Harper & Row 1956)
Dina Glouberman: *Life Choices, Life Changes through Imagework* (Unwin Hyman 1989)
John Heider: *The Tao of Leadership* (Humanics Ltd 1985)
Stephen Levine: *Healing into Life & Death* (Anchor Press/Doubleday 1987)

M. Scott Peck: *The Road Less Travelled* (Rider 1993)
Eddie & Debbie Shapiro: *A Time for Healing* (Piatkus 1995)

Native American teachings

Kenneth Meadows: *The Medicine Way* (Element 1990)

Sexuality

Margo Anand: *The Art of Sexual Ecstasy* (Aquarian 1990)
Nick Douglas & Penny Slinger: *Sexual Secrets* (Destiny Books 1979)
Mantak Chia: *Taoist Secrets of Love* (Aurora 1984)
Cultivating Female Sexual Energies (Healing Tao Books 1986)

Useful Addresses

Malcolm Stern: 'Art of Loving' and 'Courage to Love' workshops
13 Denys Road, Totnes, Devon TQ9 5TJ

For information on courses, workshops and trained practitioners:

Counselling & Psychotherapy

British Association for Counselling; 1 Regent Place,
Rugby CV21 2PJ. Phone 01788 578328
British Register of Counsellors & Psychotherapists;
PO Box 194, London SE16 1QZ. Phone 0171 237 5165
Karuna; Natsworthy Manor, Widecombe-in-the-Moor,
Newton Abbot, Devon. Phone 01647 221457
Chiron Centre; 26 Eaton Rise, London W5 2ER
Metanoia; 13 North Common Rd, Ealing Common, London W5
Minster Centre; 55–57 Minster Rd, London NW2 3SH

Centres for lectures & workshops

Alternatives; St. James's Church, 197 Piccadilly,
London W1V 0LL. Phone 0171 287 6711
Positive Living Groups; Colin Underwood, 40 Studland Rd,
Hanwell, London W7 3QX. Phone 0181 575 6480

Monkton Wyld Court; Charmouth, Bridport, Dorset DT6 6DQ.
   Phone 01297 560342
Grimstone Manor; Yelverton, Devon PL20 7QY.
   Phone 01822 854358
CAER; Rosemerryn, Lamorna, Penzance,
   Cornwall TR19 6BN. Phone 01736 810530
Ashburton Centre for Holistic Education & Training;
   79 East Street, Ashburton, S. Devon TQ13 7AL.
   Phone 01364 652784
Little Grove & Cortijo Romero; Grove Lane, Chesham,
   Buckinghamshire HP5 3QQ. Phone 01494 782720
Skyros; 92 Prince of Wales Rd, London NW5 3NE.
   Phone 0171 267 4424. (Writers' and artists' workshops;
   holidays for body, mind and spirit)

Dance workshops

Second Wave; Nappers Crossing, Staverton, Totnes,
   Devon TQ9 6PD. Phone 01803 762255

Tantric sexuality workshops

John Hawken, Lower Grumbla Farm, Newbridge, Penzance,
   Cornwall TR20 8QX. Phone 01736 788304

Index